William Pollard

The Stanleys of Knowsley

A History of that Noble Family

William Pollard

The Stanleys of Knowsley
A History of that Noble Family

ISBN/EAN: 9783337779733

Printed in Europe, USA, Canada, Australia, Japan

Cover: Foto ©ninafisch / pixelio.de

More available books at **www.hansebooks.com**

THE

STANLEYS *of* KNOWSLEY

·

A History of that Noble Family

INCLUDING

A SKETCH OF THE POLITICAL AND PUBLIC LIVES

OF THE

RIGHT HON. THE EARL OF DERBY, K.G.

AND THE

RIGHT HON. LORD STANLEY, M.P.

BY WILLIAM POLLARD.

Liverpool

EDWARD HOWELL, 26, CHURCH STREET.

1868.

HISTORY

OF THE

STANLEYS OF KNOWSLEY.

CONTENTS.

PREFACE.

As regards the earlier portions of the following pages, the author wishes it to be clearly understood that he lays no claim to originality. The records of the House of Stanley, even down to the life and times of the eleventh Earl of Derby, have been so ably penned by successive historians, that the public must already be familiar with the many heroic deeds of this illustrious family, from the time of its earliest origin; and as the author has availed himself of the several authorities at his disposal, the present volume is to some extent rather a compilation than otherwise.

A continuation of the history of the Stanleys of Knowsley has been the main object of the author, and with this end in view he has endeavoured to lay before his readers the varied interesting events connected with this ancient historical family down to the present distinguished Lord of Knowsley.

Every care has been taken to secure accuracy as regards the historical and general facts recorded in the narrative, but many omissions and defects may nevertheless be discovered. Fully sensible of its many imperfections, the author submits his work to the public, in the confident hope of its indulgent consideration.

It will be seen from the Introduction, as well as from that portion of the narrative having reference to the present Earl of Derby, that the author speaks of his Lordship in his capacity of Prime Minister; but inasmuch as the noble Earl resigned his high office whilst the work was in progress, and during its passage through the press, the event forms the subject of a special chapter.

April, 1868.

A HISTORY

OF THE

STANLEYS OF KNOWSLEY.

INTRODUCTION.

WHETHER as regards their high lineage and descent,
or the distinguished part which, for several centuries
past, they have taken in the events connected with
the political and general history of the country, it
may be safely affirmed that the "Stanleys of Knowsley" is one of the most illustrious and honoured families belonging to the British peerage. On several occasions in their history, the Stanleys have been directly
connected by marriage with royalty, and the blood of
the Plantagenets, as well as other noble families formerly allied to the crown, flows in their veins. More-

over, they for many years held regal sway in the
Isle of Man, to which we necessarily allude in
detail, in subsequent parts of our narrative.

As will be seen from what follows, the House of
Stanley, even from a period antecedent to the creation
of Thomas, the first Earl of Derby, in the year 1485,
had always been signally distinguished for its firm and
unflinching loyalty and adherence to the crown ; a
loyalty, which, on several occasions, has manifested
itself in the field, as in the case of Sir John Stanley,
(from whom the Earls of Derby descend,) who
fought near Shrewsbury, on behalf of King Henry
the Fourth, against the Earl of Northumberland
and other conspirators, and also at York, in 1405 ;
Sir Edward Stanley, who distinguished himself
in the battle of Flodden Field ; Sir William Stanley,
who, alike with Lord Stanley himself, fought
in the famous battle of Bosworth Field, when the
latter placed the crown (which had been taken from
the helmet of Richard) on the head of Henry, Earl of
Richmond ; these noble illustrations, on the part of
one family, of devoted allegiance to their king and
their country, culminating in the truly great and self-

sacrificing exploits of James, seventh Earl of Derby, who has not inappropriately been designated "the Great Stanley," and whose well known loyal and heroic devotion to King Charles, brought his lordship to the scaffold.

In later times, the descendants of the Stanleys of Knowsley have equally distinguished themselves by their services to the state and their eloquence in the senate ; and in each succeeding generation these quali-fications, on the part of the Stanleys, have been displayed by an increased and still increasing mani-festation of that genius and those great intellectual powers, which, from age to age, accompany the labours and duties of statesmanship, until in the present day, when they may be classed in the cate-gory of contemporary history, we have them brilliantly and powerfully exhibited in the persons of both sire and son, which at once command the confidence and admiration of the nation, from the felicitous and gratifying circumstance, that whilst the one is at the head of an executive, whose policy he directs and guides with a vigour and ability which has been matured by a close and lengthened experience,

the other holds a high and responsible position
in the service of the crown, in discharging the grave
and important duties of which—duties, which, at the
present critical juncture in our foreign relations, are
more than ordinarily difficult and arduous—he exhibits
an amount of talent, combined with a sagacity, care,
and self-sacrificing devotion to the interests of the
state, which have won for him the universal and
affectionate esteem of all classes and parties in
the country, who look forward with a feeling of
national pride to his elevation, at no long distant day,
to the highest office in the councils of his sovereign.

Although, however, the Stanleys of Knowsley, are
beyond question, the most illustrious and distinguished
of those who bear the name, they are not the oldest
branch, but only the second, as will be seen by the
records in succeeding pages, of the Stanley family, in
this country. As, however, the object of our present
work is mainly to chronicle the history of the Knowsley branch, and the public events connected therewith, it is unnecessary here to dwell in detail
upon the Stanleys of Hooton, in Cheshire, which
is the oldest branch; or of the Stanleys of

Alderley, in Cheshire, whose original ancestor was Sir John Stanley, the youngest son of Thomas, first Baron Stanley, father of Thomas, first Earl of Derby. Our purpose is to trace the origin, genealogy, and public career of the several members of the house of Derby, from the earliest period of its rise to the present time. The political and historical events and occurrences in which this pre-eminently noble and remarkably gifted family have prominently figured for several centuries past, are of a peculiarly interesting character, and they are rendered still more interesting, at this moment, owing to the elevated and responsible position in which the present head of the illustrious house of Stanley has now, for some time, been placed in connection with the government of the country. Events of the greatest importance, both at home and abroad, have taken place during the public life and government of the Premier who now rules in Downing Street; and as several of them form, each and respectively, an epoch in the annals of the nation with which his lordship's political career has been so closely identified, it will be seen that, in the sequel, we devote a special chapter to the consideration of this part of our subject, which cannot but be regarded as a peculiarly appropriate accompaniment to the history of the "Stanleys of Knowsley."

CHAPTER I.

ORIGIN OF THE FAMILY.

THE rise of the House of Stanley takes date so
far back as the time of William the Conqueror, for
history records that when that monarch came over to
this country, on his expedition from Normandy, he
was accompanied by one Adam de Aldithley, and
his two sons, Lydulph and Adam de Aldithley.
This family became great favourites with the King,
to whom they rendered valuable services after his
arrival in England, in return for which, his Majesty
conferred upon them extensive grants of land, and
other property and possessions. Lydulph, the eldest
son, had a son whose name again was Adam de
Aldithley. This last named Adam de Aldithley
married Mabella, the daughter of Henry Stanley de
Stoneley, who was the possessor of the extensive
manor of Stoneley and Balterley, in Staffordshire,
and this Mabella, being heiress of Henry de Stoneley,
the manor of Stoneley and Balterley came to Adam

de Aldithley, by virtue of his marriage with Mabella. William de Aldithley, who was the second son of the younger Adam de Aldithley, also married a Stanley, namely, Joan, the only daughter and heiress of Thomas Stanley, of Stafford, who was a near relative of Henry Stanley of Stoneley, whose daughter Mabella had already been married to Adam de Aldithley. By the last named marriage, the two Aldithleys, William de Aldithley and his cousin Adam, became close relatives in a double sense. By William de Aldithley's marriage with Joan, daughter and heiress of Thomas Stanley, of Stafford, he came into possession of the manor of Thalk, in Staffordshire, which Thomas Stanley presented to his daughter Joan, as a marriage portion. Sometime subsequent to the last named marriage, William de Aldithley exchanged with his cousin Adam, the manor of Thalk for that of Stoneley and one half of Balterley, and having taken up his residence at Stoneley, he assumed the surname of Stanley, and thus became the original founder of the noble family of the Stanleys of Hooton, and also, indirectly, the founder of the Stanleys of Knowsley, who are the more immediate subjects of our history. It should be here stated, that the family of Thomas Stanley, whose daughter Joan, William de Aldithley married, is reputed to have been of great antiquity, and of Saxon descent, and to have held a noble position in England for a long period before the conquest. History does not furnish us very distinctly with the direct issue of William Stanley, otherwise de Aldithley, but we find that his descendants indirectly founded the Stanleys of Hooton and Knowsley. Through the marriage of his great-grandson, Sir William Stanley, with Joan, the daughter of Sir Philip de Bamvile, whose wife was descended from Ranulph de Sylvester, Lord of Stourton, in Cheshire, the forest of Wirral, in Cheshire, came into his possession. The issue of this marriage were two sons, John and Adam Stanley, together with a daughter. The eldest son, John, became Lord Stourton, and married Mabella, daughter of Sir James Hausket, of Stourton Parva, by whom he had two sons, Sir William, his heir, and John. Sir William married Alice, daughter of Hugh Massey, of Timperley, and sister of Sir Hamon Massey, of Dunham Massey. At his death, in 1397, he left three sons, Sir William, John, and Henry, and one daughter, and it was by the marriage of the eldest son, Sir William, that the Stanleys of Hooton were founded. His wife was Margery, daughter and heiress of William de Hooton, of Hooton, in Cheshire. After his marriage, he took up his abode at Hooton Hall, which he inherited by virtue of that marriage; and his next brother, Sir John Stanley, is the direct ancestor and founder of the Stanleys of Knowsley, which, it will now be seen, is the second branch of the family; the descendants of Sir William, who were the baronets of Hooton, being, as we have already stated, the oldest branch of the family.

CHAPTER II.

HAVING already briefly sketched the earliest history of the Stanleys, from the time when their progenitors arrived in England, from Normandy, we now come to the more immediate portion of our task, namely, the History of the House of Derby, from the time of its origin in the fourteenth century; its first ancestor being, as we have already shewn, Sir John Stanley, K.G., second brother of Sir William Stanley, of Hooton. From the very earliest period of its existence, the House of Derby has occupied a prominent position amongst those which have been identified with the most striking events in the great historical records of the country. There is, perhaps, no locality better known in connection with the memorable events which signalised the civil war preceding the Commonwealth and the Restoration, than Lathom House, near Ormskirk, in Lancashire. The part which the noble and heroic Countess of

James, the seventh Earl of Derby, took at that
eventful period during the seige of Lathom, must be
well known to every reader of history. As we shall
have to devote a considerable portion of our space to
that subject when we come to record the life and
times of "the Great Stanley," it is not necessary
further to dwell upon it at present, but it is worthy
of observation, as illustrating the ancient character and
lineage of the Stanleys, that Lathom House, which,
from its remarkable and interesting historical associations, must ever hold a prominent place amongst
the records of the great and daring deeds which
distinguish the period, became the property of the
Stanleys, (and indirectly by marriage, remains in the
family still,) even in the days of their earliest ancestor
and progenitor, Sir John Stanley, who, at a comparatively early age, married Isabel, the daughter and
heiress of Sir Thomas Lathom, of Lathom and Knowsley,
and by this marriage became possessed of these now
well-known mansions and estates. John Stanley, Esq.,
(for he had not yet received the honour of knighthood) resided at Newton, near Macclesfield, in Cheshire.
He was eminently distinguished for valour in the
field. On the 19th of September, 1357, he fought
at the famous battle of Poictiers, in France, led by
Edward, the Black Prince, son of Edward the Third;
Stanley being under the command of his relation,
Lord Audley. In this battle, it will be remembered

that King John of France was taken prisoner, and brought to England. A truce having taken place, Mr. Stanley visited most of the Courts of Europe in order to improve himself in the arts of war. During this period he proved himself one of the most noted champions in single combat of the age, and on his returning to England, through France, a haughty French combatant followed him, and challenged all England to produce a person to engage him in arms. Stanley at once accepted the challenge, and, by the king's directions, the encounter took place under the walls of Winchester city, the king himself being present. Stanley was victorious, slaying his opponent, and for this act of bravery the king honoured him with knighthood, and he subsequently became a great favourite with his majesty. When Edward the Third died, Richard the Second, who succeeded him, and who also manifested a high regard for Sir John Stanley, sent him to Ireland to assist in the total reduction of that country. He was so far successful that when Richard went over he made all the great kings of Ireland do homage to him, and Ireland was reduced and subdued to the crown of England; and for his services there the king, in 1385, appointed him Lord Deputy of Ireland, accompanied by a grant of the manor and lands of Blake Castle in that country. When King Richard was deposed, on the

20th of September, 1399, and King Henry the
Fourth came to the throne, his majesty being well
aware of Sir John Stanley's great power and influence
in the kingdom, took him into his favour, and
granted him large possessions in Cheshire. He also
continued him in his office as Lord Lieutenant of
Ireland for six years. The king, however, had not
been long on the throne before his enemies began
to conspire against him, and went so far as to plot
against his life. At the head of one of these con-
spiracies were the Percys, Earls of Northumberland
and Worcester, together with the Earl of March, and
one Owen Glendower, of Wales, who entered into a
triple league, offensive and defensive, whereby it
was agreed that England and Wales should be
divided into three parts, to be placed under the
government of the several conspirators. On this
becoming known to the king, he called Sir John
Stanley from Ireland, and immediately appointed
him steward of his household, and by Sir John's
advice and assistance a considerable army was raised,
which the King headed himself, his son and Sir John
being under him, and with them marched against
the rebels. Near Shrewsbury they met and engaged
the enemy, and after a determined battle, the fighting
being furious on both sides, the king was victorious,
Sir John Stanley, who eminently distinguished himself on this critical occasion, materially contributing

towards the victory. The Earl of Northumberland was killed, the Earl of Worcester taken prisoner and beheaded, and 6000 were slain on the field. Shortly after this, in 1405, Sir John received a commission to seize upon the Isle of Man, which had been forfeited by Henry Percy, Earl of Northumberland, and this commission, which Sir John received along with one Roger Leke, also extended to the city of York, and its liberties, the king having been informed that the city, castle, and precincts of York still held out for the deposed King Richard, then a prisoner in Pomfret Castle. In the following year, 1406, Sir John obtained a license from his majesty to fortify a spacious house he was then building at Liverpool, with embattled walls. In reference to this house, Seacome says, "which, when finished he called the Tower; being ever since well known by that name, and is now (1793) standing in good order." He also further says, that Lady Stanley, the widow of Sir William, "did, on the death of Sir John, her husband, return, with her children, from Ireland to Liverpool, and lived in the house erected there by Sir John, called the tower." In consideration of the great services which he had rendered to the king, his majesty, on the 6th of April, 1407, granted the Isle of Man to Sir John Stanley, and his heirs for ever, and that the next year placed him in full possession of the Isle of Man, with nothing less than

regal and kingly sway, having obtained a grant of the
Island, together with the castle, formerly called
Holm Town, as well as the adjoining isles, with the
regalias, franchises, and other large privileges, " to be
" holden of the said King, his heirs and successors, by
" homage, and the service of two falcons, payable on
" the days of their coronation." He continued in favour
with the King up to the time of his Majesty's death,
and on Henry the Fifth coming to the throne,
the royal approbation was maintained, for on the
King's accession he was created a Knight of the
Garter, and was also made Lord Lieutenant of Ireland
for a period of six years. He died on the 6th of
January, 1414, whilst still fulfilling the office of
Lord Lieutenant. He left behind him, at his death,
six children, namely—four sons and two daughters.
The eldest son was Sir John, who of course succeeded
his father. Henry was the second, Thomas the third,
and Ralph was the fourth.

Sir John Stanley, the eldest son, and heir of the
first ancestor of the " Stanleys of Knowsley," did not
take any very prominent part in the public affairs of
the nation, but like his immediate progenitor, he was
true to the King, and received, during his lifetime,
several marks of the royal favour. For many years
he was a Knight of the Shire, and during the

reign of Henry the Sixth, he held the office of Constable of Carnarvon Castle, an office which, at that period, was considered to be one of high honour. At the same time he also held the office of Justice of Chester, and, during the same king's reign was Sheriff of Anglesey. He married Isabel, the daughter of Sir John, and sister and heiress of Sir William Harrington, Knight, of Hornby, near Lancaster, Lancashire, and the eldest son by this marriage, Sir Thomas, became first Baron Stanley, this Sir John, therefore, being grandfather to Thomas, the first Earl of Derby. Besides Thomas, the first Baron Stanley, Sir John had also two other sons, Richard and Edward. Both these sons went into the Church, and held high positions in it. Being closely connected with the County Palatine, the influence of the family led to their promotion, and they were each in turn made Archdeacon of Chester, Richard being the first Archdeacon, and at his death, his brother Edward was appointed to the vacant office. Sir John died in 1444.

Sir Thomas Stanley, son and heir of Sir John, and first Lord Stanley, obtained the title by the favour of the crown, to which, like his predecessors, he was warmly devoted. Having been for many years Knight of the Shire, he was summoned to the House

of Peers on the 20th of January, 1456, being the 34th
year of the reign of Henry the Sixth. He held the
office of Lord Lieutenant for six years, but subsequent
to that period he was essentially a courtier, having for
several years held the office of Comptroller of the
Household, and Chamberlain to his Majesty. His lordship married a lady of the highest lineage, which allied
the Stanleys directly to royalty. This lady was
Joan, daughter and co-heiress of Sir Robert Goushill,
of Heveringham, in the county of Nottinghamshire, by
Elizabeth, his wife. The last named lady was the
widow of Thomas Mowbray, Duke of Norfolk, and
daughter and co-heiress of Richard Fitzalan, Earl of
Arundel, by Elizabeth, his wife, daughter of William
Bohun, Earl of Hereford and Essex, by his wife,
Princess Elizabeth Plantagenet, daughter of King
Edward the First. It will thus be seen that the first
Baron Stanley formed an alliance which brought the
Knowsley family into immediate relationship with
the blood royal of the day. The issue of this marriage
were four sons and two daughters. The eldest son,
Thomas, ultimately became the first Earl of Derby.
The other sons were Sir William, of Holt Castle, in
Denbighshire, whose life was forfeited on the scaffold,
on a charge of conspiracy, made, however, by a self-
accused accomplice, and upon which we shall more fully
dwell in a future stage of our history. We may however
here remark, briefly, that the devotion and bravery

manifested by Sir William to the royal cause, at the battle of Bosworth Field, renders the charge of his having subsequently been engaged in a conspiracy against the King, highly improbable. The third son was Sir John, who married Elizabeth, daughter of Sir Thomas Weever, of Weever, in Cheshire, and by this marriage he obtained the Weever estates, and became the founder of the Stanleys of Alderley, the present Baron who sits in the House of Peers, being Edward John, second Lord Stanley, of Alderley. The youngest son was James, who entered the Church, and became Archdeacon of Carlisle. His lordship died in the year 1400.

————

Thomas, the first Earl of Derby, succeeded his father as Lord Stanley, in 1460, but was only elevated to the earldom 25 years afterwards, shortly after the close of the famous battle of Bosworth Field, in which his lordship took a distinguished and prominent part against the tyrant Richard, Duke of Gloucester, fighting on the side of the Earl of Richmond afterwards Henry the Seventh. It may, without any exaggeration be stated that the splendid career of the first Earl of Derby, and his daring and bravery in the field, when Lord Stanley, marks one of the brightest pages in English History, of which the Stanleys of

Knowsley may well feel proud. He, like his immediate ancestors, was devotedly attached to the crown, and manifested a fervent spirit of loyalty in all the great historical events in which he took part. It was in the first year of Edward the Fourth that he was summoned to Parliament, and about that period he allied himself in marriage with Eleanor, daughter of the Earl of Salisbury, and sister to the Earl of Warwick, who was popularly known as the "King-making Earl." His lot being cast in the days of the "Wars of the Roses," he espoused the cause of the House of York, although his relative, the Earl of Warwick, when he threw off his allegiance to King Edward, and joined the Lancastrians, made overtures to Lord Stanley to join him in that cause, but his lordship's loyalty to the crown was strong enough to make him resist the temptation. By this marriage he had six sons, the exploits of one of whom—the fifth, Edward—we shall have to notice in a subsequent portion of our history. His first wife died several years after the marriage, and subsequently he contracted a second marriage with a lady of the most exalted rank—Margaret of Lancaster, mother of Henry the Seventh. This royal lady had already been twice married, and at the time of her marriage with Lord Stanley, she was a widow in a double sense. Her first husband was Edmund, Earl of Richmond, who died in about a year after the marriage,

namely, in 1456. Her second marriage was with
Henry Stafford, second son of Humphrey, Duke of
Buckingham, who also died in a very few years after
the nuptials. The circumstances attendant upon the
royal lady's last marriage, with Lord Stanley, are of a
somewhat extraordinary and romantic character, and
are thus graphically described by an eminent historian
of the House of Stanley :—

"Her third marriage," says the writer, "with Lord
" Stanley, was anything but a love match—rather what
" the French call a *marriage de convenance*, contracted
" solely from prudential motives. The Countess, who
" was distinguished for a rigour of devotion, uncommon
" even in those times, had made a vow, after the death of
" her second husband, never to admit a third to her bed,
" and Stanley coolly assented to this very singular
" condition previous to the marriage—if such it can be
" called. It requires no sketch of fancy to conceive
" that the 'baked meats' served up at the celebration
" of this *unique* compact—

'Did coldly furnish forth the marriage table.'

" It is surely needless to add, that the peerage
" records no 'issue' as the result of this strange matri-
" monial conjunction—the only one of the kind, we
" presume, that has ever yet been recorded in the
" history of the human race. Like the famous
" ancestors of the Earls of Dalhousie, 'the laird o'

" Cockpen,' the noble Stanley certainly had for his
" bride, so far as rank and title were concerned—

                      'a weel tappit hen,
      'But nae chickens at all had the laird o' Cockpen.'

" To judge from his portrait now before us, he
" looks—with his bonnet perched upon his lofty brow,
" his keen bright eye, and his flowing beard—one of the
" very last whom we should have suspected to be guilty
" of such atrocious self-denial. The Countess, whose
" portrait is also in our possession, is drawn with
" uplifted hands in the attitude of prayer—her breviary
" laid open on the cushion before her. She is arrayed
" in the muffled habit of a religionist, and looks the
" incarnation of a saint already half exhaled ; and we
" dare pledge our creed upon the fact that she not
" only made the vow of continence ascribed to her, but
" kept it into the bargain. Indeed, it is said to be yet
" extant in the archives of St. John's College, Cambridge,
" which she founded. If so, we trust it will never be
" exhumed, and published as a formula for the
" adoption of the sex—or, as the poet happily
" expresses it—

      'For general subscription by the ladies.'

" It was administered by her chaplain and confessor,
" the wise, learned, pious, and candid John Fisher."

    During a considerable portion of the reign of
Edward, Lord Stanley was attached to the royal house-

hold, and largely enjoyed the King's favour, having
filled, amongst other offices, that of Steward of the
Household. In the Civil War which raged, he performed several acts of valour, during the time he was
commanding the army in Scotland, and amongst his
achievements, at this time, he took the town of
Berwick by assault.

After Edward's death, which happened shortly
after Lord Stanley's marriage to Henry the Seventh's
mother, the designs of Richard, the usurper, excited
the deadly hostility of Lord Stanley; and, along
with others, he determined, if possible, to bring
about the downfall of the tyrant; but his plans for
effecting this object, as well as those of Richmond,
with whom he was intimately associated in the project,
were, from prudential motives, kept as secret as
possible. There is, however, every reason to believe
that his intentions came to the knowledge of Richard,
for the year after Stanley had commanded in Scotland, he
had a narrow escape of his life at a council which was
held in the Tower, when Lord Hastings was arrested
and lost his life. On this occasion, one of Richard's
soldiers struck Lord Stanley on the head with a pole-
axe, and the wound, which was a severe one, had well
nigh been fatal. Richard pretended that it was an
accident, but this was not believed, and there can be
little doubt, if historical records are reliable, that the
tyrant intended his lordship's death, which subsequent

events, indeed, render certain. Although Lord Stanley, on this occasion, received serious wounds, he was arrested and imprisoned on a charge of conspiracy. Events which happened shortly afterwards, however, gave an entire change to the aspect of affairs. Richard knew and felt the power and influence of Lord Stanley, and therefore feared him as much as he hated him.

In little more than a month after the arrest of Lord Stanley, Richard was suddenly and unexpectedly elevated to the throne, when, in order no doubt to cajole his lordship, the usurper not only released him from imprisonment, but heaped dignities upon him, including that of appointing him High Constable of England, and he also conferred upon him the Order of the Garter. Not only so, but Lord Stanley's lady was selected to bear the train at the coronation of the usurper's Queen. The sequel disclosed the truth, that all these honours, suddenly offered to Stanley, originated in the tyrant's mind out of duplicity and deception engendered by fear, and that Richard had in reality, no good feeling whatever towards Stanley. It subsequently transpired, that his eldest son, Lord Strange (this title he assumed by virtue of his marriage with the heiress of that barony) was organising a powerful force on his Lincolnshire estates, to oppose Richard; and the latter, by offering favours to Lord Strange's father, indulged the hope of winning him over; but in this he was altogether mistaken, for, as the result proved, Stanley became Richard's deadliest enemy; the suspicious, sudden, and mysterious disappearance of the young princes having hastened the final event. Their death led the Duke of Buckingham, who was originally in favour of Richard, to suggest that the crown should be transferred to Henry, Earl of Richmond, and this proposal was eagerly adopted, Lord Stanley readily throwing himself into the cause of Richmond, assisted by his brother, Sir William Stanley. The two brothers marched an army of their dependents, numbering upwards of six thousand, in the direction of Lichfield, and were at the same time in constant communication with Richmond, who was in advance, after landing in Wales. It was in a field in the village of Atherstone, near Tamworth, where the leaders of Richmond's party met to consult how they could best give battle to the tyrant, this meeting being secret and unobserved. Meanwhile, Richard had already arrested Lord Strange, as a hostage for the fidelity of his father, and the latter was naturally in a state of considerable anxiety as to the safety of his son, who was a prisoner in Richard's camp. Notwithstanding, however, the peril in which he knew his son was placed, whilst in the power of the tyrant, he was at the same time most anxious for the success and triumph of Richmond. The battle was arranged for the following day, August 22nd, 1485, and a short

time before it commenced he received a message from
Richard, stating, that if he did not instantly join him in
the field he would decapitate Lord Strange, and this
message was accompanied by the tyrant's oath, that it
would certainly be carried out. Lord Stanley returned
for his answer the following concise and expressive
reply, "I have more sons, and cannot come." Immediately afterwards the decisive battle commenced, Lord
Stanley and his brother—at first, with their men, but
spectators of the fight—ultimately fighting side by side
for Richmond, the result being Richard's downfall and
death, and Richmond's triumph. As regards Lord
Strange, Richard would have carried out his threat, had
he not been dissuaded from it by some of those around
him, for historians add, that the tyrant, as he had
sworn to do, ordered the Lord Strange to be beheaded at the instant the two armies were to engage,
but some of his council told him "now was the
time to fight, and not to execute," and the Lord
Strange was remanded to the tents until the battle
was over. There is a difference amongst historians
as to whether, after the battle, Lord Stanley or his
brother, Sir William, placed the crown which was
taken from Richard's helmet, on the head of Richmond, but we are inclined to think that the balance
of evidence is in favour of the act having been performed by the former. This memorable battle was
followed by the "Union of the Roses," Henry the

Seventh of Lancaster, having on the 18th of January, 1486, married Elizabeth, the "White Rose," of York, daughter of King Edward; and thus, by the death of the last of the Plantagenets, was brought to a termination that deadly struggle between the Houses of York and Lancaster, which had extended over a period of three decades, deluged England with blood, and cost more than a hundred thousand lives.

On the 30th of October, 1485, the day of Henry's coronation, Lord Stanley was created Earl of Derby, and filled several great offices of State, and in 1496, he went on a diplomatic mission to the court of France. He died in the year 1504, and was buried at Burscough Abbey, near Ormskirk. Some slight remains of this Abbey, which is situate within the Lathom desmesne, and which was founded by the Earl's ancestors, are still preserved. His lordship had six sons and four daughters, all, of course, by his first wife. His second, who survived him five years, was interred in one of the chapels in Westminster Abbey.

We have already referred to the ignominious death of Sir William Stanley, who fought with his brother, the Earl, then Lord Stanley, at the battle of Bosworth. After the bravery and devoted loyalty which he displayed towards Richmond on that memorable battle field, it is almost impossible to believe that he could be guilty of the crime which, ten years afterwards, was laid to his charge. But

so it was that early in the year 1495, he was charged
with assisting in a conspiracy to place Perkin Warbeck on the throne. As regards this pretender, or
rather tool, it should be stated that in the year 1493,
the Duchess of Burgundy, sister to King Edward the
Fourth, and an inveterate enemy to King Henry and
the House of Lancaster, disturbed his peace by setting up one Perkin Warbeck, to personate and take
upon himself to be Richard, the younger son of
Edward the Fourth. Several of the enemies of the
king supported the duchess in this matter, and entered into a conspiracy to depose King Henry.
Amongst them was Sir Robert Clifford, who, on the
conspiracy being discovered, in order to save his own
life, confessed to having been concerned in it, as the
chief conspirator, and at the same time charged Sir
William Stanley with being his principal abettor, and
on this charge he was arrested and tried. Sir Robert
Clifford, being his accuser, stated openly in the
council, that in a conversation with Sir William Stanley on the subject, Sir William remarked,
"that if he certainly knew the young man, called
"Perkin Warbeck, to be really the son of Edward the
"Fourth, he would never draw his sword or bear arms
"against him." This, even, according to Clifford himself, was all the evidence against Sir William. When
the charge was made King Henry *appeared* to dis-
believe it altogether, stating, that it was impossible

to impute treason to a man who had so nobly fought for him, and to whom, indeed, he was indebted for the very crown he wore; a man to whom he had felt it his duty, on every consideration of gratitude, to express his deepest thankfulness; a man, moreover, whose brother, the Earl of Derby, was his own step-father; a man to whom he had even entrusted his person, as his lord chamberlain. The charge, however, was persistently maintained by Clifford, and what renders the whole subject more extraordinary and mysterious is, that when Sir William was called upon to answer the accusation, he neither denied nor acknowledged his guilt. The course he adopted astonished and bewildered those present at the time, as well it might; but it is far from improbable, judging from his antecedents, that he felt too indignant to reply, believing, possibly, that his accuser would be discredited, and that he would be instantly and honourably acquitted. Unfortunately, however, he was condemned to death, and the sentence was carried out, the unhappy knight being beheaded at Tower Hill, on the 16th of February. It might reasonably be supposed that a self-accused conspirator would have been discredited; and, in the relative position in which he was placed towards Sir William, it might have been expected that the king would not have carried out the sentence, but his Majesty, we are told, was "a mean and avaricious man," and us

Sir William was very wealthy, being possessed of upwards of £3000 per annum in landed property, and 40,000 marks in plate and money, besides other property of great value, which was afterwards discovered at his mansion, Holt Castle, when his effects, confiscated to the crown, were seized, the forfeiture of this is said to have acted as a powerful motive for the course which the king adopted.

Notwithstanding the sad fate of his brother, to which the king was thus a party, the loyalty of the earl was unshaken, and his subsequent conduct shewed great magnanimity. In a few months after Sir William was executed, namely, on the 24th of June, Henry the Seventh paid a visit to his stepfather, at Knowsley and Lathom, spending a month with the earl, by whom he was entertained on a scale of princely hospitality; and in order to shew the self sacrificing loyalty and devotion of the earl, even in the deep affliction under which he must have been suffering at the untimely death of his brother, it may be stated that the moment he received the intimation of the intended royal visit, he set about enlarging and decorating both Lathom and Knowsley, in order to entertain his Majesty in a manner becoming his position as king.

Seacome, after commenting with much severity on the king's conduct in this matter, says that at the battle of Bosworth the chances were going against

Richmond, until Sir William Stanley brought 3000 horse and foot into the field, and then asks "How "could it then enter into his head or heart to put him "to death who had done for him all that mortality "could do? Satisfied his life, vanquished his enemies, "and given him a crown, and all his crime founded upon "a doubtful and unguarded expression, reported by a "treacherous friend, a rebel, and a traitor to his king, "by his own confession to save his own life; and "therefore should have been the less regarded, when "the duty, loyalty, and most worthy actions of so "deserving a subject were in competition with it."

In connexion with this royal visit, a story of an amusing character is told, which is as follows:— When the King visited Lathom, the Earl, after his royal guest had viewed the whole house, conducted him up to the leads for a prospect of the country. The Earl's fool, who was among the company, observing the King draw near to the edge, not guarded by a balustrade, stepped up to the Earl, and pointing down to the precipice, said, "Tom, remember Will." The King perfectly appreciated the meaning of the remark, and made a precipitate retreat down stairs, and out of the house; and the fool, for some-time afterwards, was grievously mortified that his lord had not had the courage to take the opportunity of avenging himself for the death of his brother.

In the year 1513, the earl's fifth son, Edward,

performed prodigies of valour at the battle of Flodden Field, being in charge of the left wing of the English army. The English arrows were so fearfully effective on the extreme right of the Scottish army, that a body of Highlanders broke their ranks, and rushed in disorder down hill. Sir Edward Stanley, with the men of Lancashire and Cheshire, attacked them both in flank and rear, and they were routed with terrible slaughter. At the same moment, however, the Scottish troops led on by their King, were making sad havoc among the main body of the English army, which was under the command of the Earl of Surrey, and for a time the fortune of war was in favour of the Scotch. But Sir Edward Stanley came up on one flank of the King's division, after defeating the Highlanders, and the Scottish troops being also attacked on the other side, " the gallant monarch fell, with the flower of his nobility." Sir Walter Scott's allusion to Sir Edward, in *Marmion*, will be familiar to every one—

" Charge, Chester, charge !—On, Stanley, on !"

In the following year, Sir Edward had the title of Baron Monteagle conferred upon him, in recognition of his signal services at Flodden; but it fell into abeyance about the commencement of the seventeenth century, and was only revived some years ago, when it was conferred upon Mr. Spring Rice, a member of a former whig administration.

CHAPTER III.

THOMAS, SECOND EARL, TO WILLIAM, SIXTH EARL OF DERBY.

Lord Strange, who was held captive by Richard, during the battle of Bosworth Field, was of course released when the tyrant was defeated. He had issue by his marriage, besides daughters, two sons, the eldest of whom, Thomas, became the second Earl of Derby, his father, the son of the first Earl, dying in the year 1497; the second Earl of Derby, therefore, succeeding his grandfather, who died, as has been already stated, in 1504. Beyond his being a courtier, there is nothing particularly noteworthy in the Earl's career. He was a confidant of King Henry, and accompanied him in the several expeditions which he undertook, and being a member of his Majesty's household, he carried the royal sword between the Emperor Charles the Fifth, and King Henry the Eighth, from Dover to Canterbury, in the year 1520, on the occasion of the first named monarch visiting this country. Candour compels us to say

3

that a dark cloud hangs over his memory, but it is gratifying to be able to add, that it is the only blot upon the otherwise brilliant escutcheon of the Derby family. In the present age, a trial in which the noble Earl was engaged, would not be tolerated, and we must therefore regard, with considerable forbearance, the peculiar circumstances in which he was placed. The facts are simple, and are only interesting in so far as they serve to illustrate the singular incredulity of the time. It is recorded, that Edward Stafford, the last Duke of Buckingham, in that line of the family, had been led to believe by an astrologer, that he was next in succession to the throne. For the part he took in this singularly romantic delusion, he was tried before a jury of his peers, the Earl of Derby being one of them. The other members of the jury consisted of a duke, a marquis, seven earls, and twelve barons, the Duke of Norfolk being president; and it is a remarkable fact, as illustrating the extraordinary self-sacrificing character of the time, that the Earl of Surrey, son of the Duke of Norfolk, had married the daughter of the very Duke of Buckingham, who was then before his peers on a trial in which his life or death was the issue. It might have been supposed, in the case of the Duke, that parental affection would have prevailed, by his interposition with his brother peers, but the result proved it to be otherwise. Buckingham was condemned for the offence, and expiated his then considered crime on the scaffold. In an enlightened age like the present, it is difficult to believe in the reality of such a proceeding, but we only record what history has given us, and the moral must be left to our readers. The subject of our notice, Thomas, the second Earl of Derby, married Anne, daughter of Edward, Lord Hastings and Hungerford. It is not unworthy of record, that his death took place in ten days after that of his brother peer, the Duke of Buckingham, to whose ignominious end the Earl had been a party. The second Earl of Derby died on the 23rd of May, 1521, and was succeeded by his son Edward. During his life time he gave up the title of "King" for "Lord" of the Isle of Man.

The reigns of Mary and Elizabeth, in which the third Earl of Derby lived, as well as in the time of Henry the Eighth and Edward the Sixth, were distinguished as well as disgraced by many occurrences in the history of those eventful times. It is no part of our present task to make any passing remarks on the questionable, not to say the indiscreet, favouritism which the latter always evinced towards the Earl of Leicester. It may safely be left to the judgment of posterity to pronounce upon that much disputed point, but there can be no question that in many respects, she dignified and adorned the crown which she wore. Both Queens, like the two kings who preceded them, were in accord in their recognition and appreciation of Edward, the third Earl of Derby. The career of this Earl was contemporaneous with all the dazzling court brilliancies which characterised that period in the history of the country. The great Cardinal Wolsey was then in the zenith of his fame, and the Earl of Derby appears to have been desirous even to eclipse him in his external magnificent displays. He was a prominent actor on the occasion when King Henry had an interview with the French King, in 1532; and when Anne Boleyn came to London, on the occasion of her coronation, the Earl of Derby received her at Greenwich, and brought her thence to London in his own barge. In after years he was equally popular with the crown, and the Order of the Garter, which, down to the present day has scarcely ever been separated from the Derby family, was bestowed by King Edward on the third Earl. When Queen Mary was crowned, the Earl of Derby was Lord Steward, and, in order to be present at her coronation, he travelled from the family mansion at Knowsley, in almost regal state. The expenses of the cavalcade must have been enormous, for, unlike the present day, there were then no railways, and his lordship and his retinue had to travel by road. The attendants who accompanied his lordship on this occasion are said to have consisted of upwards of four score in velvet, and between two and three hundred in livery. He was also very popular with "Good Queen Bess," who reposed so much confidence in him, that she was in the habit of deputing to him the duty of administering the Oath of Supremacy.

In his hospitalities, the noble Earl was unequalled in the princely liberality which he was in the habit of displaying, and it has been said of him, by one of his biographers, that "with Edward, Earl of Derby's death, the glory of hospitality seemed to fall asleep." In proof of his loyalty and devotion to the throne and the constitution, it is also recorded that he offered ten thousand men, at his own cost, to suppress the last rebellion; "meat, drink, money, and money's worth, to two thousand, every Good Friday, for five and thirty years; feeding the aged, in number, three score and ten, twice a day, besides all comers thrice a week; and, what is by no means to be omitted, 'his cunning in setting bones, disjointed or broken, his surgery, and desire to help the poor!'" The Earl at the ancient family seat in Lancashire, had around him the enormous number of two hundred and fifty servants. In reference to his tenantry, he studiously adhered to the principle of never raising the rents of any of them, a principle which seems to have animated each succeeding Earl, for we have reasons to know that the present Earl, most religiously enforces upon his agents the obligation of never advancing the rents of any of the tenants who occupied lands or tenements belonging to him at the period when he succeeded to the Earldom. The Earl was three times married, his first wife being Dorothy, second daughter of the Duke of Norfolk ; and, dying on the 24th of October, 1572, he was succeeded by his son Henry, by his first wife. The Earl's funeral took place with unusual pomp and ceremony. He was the first of the family buried at Ormskirk.

The fourth Earl of Derby, Henry, did not distinguish himself in any way worthy of the great fame of his ancestors, and we have, therefore, little to say in reference to his public or private career. By his marriage he became connected with the blood royal, having been united with Margaret, daughter of Henry Clifford, second Earl of Cumberland, by his first marriage with Eleanor, daughter and co-heiress of Charles Brandon, Duke of Suffolk, and Mary, Queen Dowager of France, youngest sister of King Henry the Eighth. The only notable events in the life-time of the Earl are two, and we are bound to confess, if history does not err, that in one of them he does not appear to advantage. He was one of the peers on the occasion of the trial of Mary Queen of Scots, but there is no feature in that otherwise memorable historical event, which calls for any special remark. He was, however, also Lord High Steward

on the occasion of the trial of Philip Howard, Earl of
Arundel, who, having been prosecuted in the Star
Chamber, and fined £10,000, and imprisonment
"during the Queen's pleasure"—which was for four
years—for "entertaining Romish priests in his family,"
was afterwards brought to trial in Westminster Hall,
in April, 1589, on fresh charges, "none of which," it
is recorded, "could be substantiated, except that of his
being reconciled to the Church of Rome, and on that
ground alone was he found guilty, and condemned to
death. A prosecution so flagrant disgusted the whole
body of the peerage, twentyfive only of the most
abject of whom appeared to sit in judgment on him.
Over these, the Earl of Derby presided." He was
condemned but not executed, and after an imprisonment of three years, died, it was supposed, by
poison, on the 19th October, 1595. Queen Elizabeth, during the whole of the proceedings, evinced
a bitter hatred towards him. The chronicle of
his death says, speaking of the Earl of Derby, "by a
strange retribution he was preceded to the grave by
the judge who so unjustly condemned him." The
Earl of Derby died on the 25th of September, 1592,
having left, as his successor, (besides other sons and
daughters) Ferdinand, who became the fifth Earl.

Ferdinand the fifth Earl of Derby, who only lived
two years to enjoy the honours incident to the Earldom,

was more distinguished for his fragmentary literary productions than for any other marks of distinction. In early life he married Alice, daughter of Sir John Spencer, of Althorp, in Northamptonshire, an ancestor of the present Earl Spencer. The issue of this marriage were three daughters, but no sons. During the Earl's lifetime, a man named Hacket, an agent of the Jesuits, was convicted of treason, having been brought to trial, chiefly at the instance of his lordship, and it is believed that the part which the Earl of Derby took in this transaction, led to his lordship being poisoned, and that one of the Earl's attendants was bribed to carry out the deed. Referring to the subject, Camden, in his memorials of the Stanley family, when speaking of the Earl, says, "he died in the flower of his youth, not without suspicion of poison; no small suspicion lighted on the gentleman of his horse, who, as soon as the Earl took to his bed, took his best horse and fled." The Earl died on the 16th of April, 1594.

Ferdinand, the fifth Earl, having died without male issue, was succeeded by his brother, William, as sixth Earl. He married into an ancient family, his wife being Elizabeth, daughter of Edward Vere, seventeenth Earl of Oxford. Not long after he succeeded to the earldom, he turned his attention to the Isle of

Man, in which the family had now for so many
years held sway. He came into possession of the
Lordship of the Isle, by virtue of a purchase from the
co-heirs of his brother, which was ratified by parliament, and the crown gave him a new grant of the
island. The manner in which his lordship conducted
himself gained for him a large amount of respect, as
will be seen from the following facts: "James the
"First, whose eldest son, Henry, had been created
"Earl of Chester, a title which, after his death, had
"been conferred on Charles, his second son, visited the
"county in 1617, in great state, being attended by
"many honourable earls, reverend bishops, and worthy
"knights and courtiers, besides all the gentry of the
"shire. He was received at Chester with every mark
"of loyalty, by the mayor and officers of the city, who,
"after a series of entertainments, presented him with
"'a fair standing cup, having a covering doubly gilt,
"and therein one hundred jacobins of gold.' Among
"the parties in attendance was William, Earl of Derby,
"who was then Chamberlain of the Palatine." The
Stanleys, as we have already seen, had long been
connected with Cheshire, and had enjoyed many
offices of the highest distinction. Upon every occasion the citizens of Chester were anxious to show
their respect to the members of a family that had so
greatly contributed to their welfare; accordingly, in
the Harleian MSS. it is recorded that, "on the 18th

"September, 1630, there came to Chester, being on
" a Saturday, the Duchess of Tremoyle in France, and
" mother-in-law to the Lord Strange, and many other
" great estates; and all the gentry of Cheshire, Flint-
" shire, and Denbighshire went to meet her at Hoole
" Heath, with the Earl of Derby, being at least six
" hundred men; all the gentlemen of the artelery yard,
" lately erected at Chester, met her in Cow Lane, in
" very stately manner, all with great white and blew
" fithers, and went before her chariot to the bishop's
" pallas, and making a yard, let her through the midst,
" and there gave her three volleys of shot, and so
" returned to their yard; also, the maior and aldermen,
" in their best gowns and aparel, were on a stage in
" the Eastgate to entertayn her."

The Earl, who spent his time chiefly in Knowsley,
the Isle of Man, and Bidston in Cheshire, was
very domesticated in his habits, rarely taking any
active part in public life, although he was very
regular in his attendance as a Peer of Parliament.
We should say that Bidston Hall was built by the
Earl, soon after he succeeded to the title and estates
of his brother Ferdinand. William, at the death of his
brother, was abroad, and after his return he had much
difficulty in vindicating his claim to the estates,
against the pretensions of the daughters of the deceased Earl. Having, in consequence, passed many
years in a state of contention foreign to his character

and disposition, as soon as he arrived in England, and was finally seated in his possessions, he surrendered the cares and duties of his property to his son James, and retired for the summer to Bidston, which the old chroniclers say, "he affected very much." He also resided very much at Chester, being Lord Lieutenant and Chamberlain of the county, and died at Chester, on the 29th of September, 1642, being succeeded by James, "The Great Stanley," whose memorable career and unfortunate death we shall now proceed to narrate.

CHAPTER IV.

JAMES, SEVENTH EARL OF DERBY.

JAMES, "The Great Stanley," and seventh Earl of Derby, who succeeded his father, William, the sixth Earl, bore the title of Lord Strange up to the time of his father's death. When Charles the First ascended the throne, the then Lord Strange, the subject of our notice, was a young man, and was among the large number of those who were made Knights of the Bath, on the occasion of Charles's coronation. In early life he formed an exalted alliance with the French royal family, marrying Charlotte de la Tremouille, third daughter of Claude, Duke of Thouars, Prince of Palmont, and a peer of France, who was descended maternally through a Princess of Orange, from the royal house of Montpensier. By this union the Earl had a numerous family. In his younger days he was, like his father, domesticated in his habits and tastes, and spent his time mainly at Lathom and Knowsley, freely mingling with the tenantry on the estates and the population

of the immediate neighbourhood; relieved only by
frequent visits to the Isle of Man, where the Derby
family then reigned in truly regal state.   His father,
the sixth earl, who was at this time still living, had, as
we have already stated, handed over the management
and superintendence of the family estates, both in
Lancashire and the Isle of Man, to Lord Strange,
and it was while his lordship was living in the retirement to which we have alluded, that the civil war
broke out, and Lord Strange at once espoused the
cause of the King in opposition to the Parliament.
Warrington was the locality which Charles, at the
commencement of the war, fixed upon for his head
quarters, and the King, having called upon the several
counties to assist him in the struggle against the
Parliamentary forces, Lord Strange was placed at the
head of the counties of Lancashire, Cheshire, and
North Wales, as Lord Lieutenant, and he at once
entered upon the arduous task of raising the royal
forces in these different counties.

Having got together several thousand men, Lord
Strange marched them in the direction of Manchester,
a town, which, on the first outbreak of the war,
manifested a desire, on the part of several of its
inhabitants, to espouse the cause of the parliament.
Having called upon the inhabitants to lay down their
arms, and deliver up their magazines, a demand which
was not complied with, an engagement took place

between the royal forces and the residents, in which
eleven of the latter were killed, but his lordship had
the worst of the encounter, and, after losing thirty of
his men, he retreated from the attack.   Notwithstanding, however, the defeat of Lord Strange, on the
occasion just referred to, it must not be supposed that
the whole of the inhabitants were hostile to the royal
cause.   On the contrary, only a few days after this
encounter, a number of influential persons amongst
the loyal party in that town invited his lordship to a
public dinner, which he accepted; but while the
entertainment was in progress, it was ascertained that
Captain Holcroft and Captain Birch, at the head of
the opposite forces, had entered the town.   His
lordship immediately left the banquetting room, and
in a few moments, being at the head of upwards of
four hundred of his troops, an engagement took place
between the opposing parties, in the course of which
a man named Percival was killed by the royalists,
who had the best of the encounter.   Having been so
far successful at Manchester, his lordship extended
his operations to other parts of the county, namely,
to Preston, Ormskirk, and Bury; and it would
appear almost incred'ble, but is nevertheless undoubtedly true, as we learn from several historical
records, all in agreement with each other, that in each
of these three towns, not less than 20,000 men came
forward to support the King's cause on the call of

his lordship, being 60,000 men altogether; and these men having been fully armed and made ready to take the field, his lordship set about raising a like number of men, if possible, in the county of Chester, and the neighbouring counties in North Wales. But an extraordinary communication, which mortified and wounded him much, had the effect of materially interfering with the execution of this project. The manner in which he was treated on this occasion evinced much ingratitude on the part of the council, which denounced what they called his "noisy musters,"—the " pre-indication of his own ambitious designs," and he was actually deprived of the lieutenancy of Chester and North Wales. At the same time he was informed that the King had determined to set up his standard at Nottingham, and this communication was accompanied by one direct from the King, who desired him to push forward with as many troops as he could completely arm and equip. This intimation had a most depressing effect on his lordship, for it not only seriously interfered with his intentions and designs on behalf of the King, but it had also the effect of separating from him great numbers of those whom he had been able to collect on behalf of the royal cause in Preston, Ormskirk, and Bury, many of whom returned to their homes, determining to take no further part on the side of the King or of Parliament, whilst large bodies went

over to the side of the Parliamentary forces, and
actually aided them in obtaining possession of Manchester. It is not a little interesting, as showing his
devotion to the King, in the face of these adverse
circumstances, that he managed to raise and equip
three regiments of cavalry, and three of foot; and
having done so, he repaired to Shrewsbury, where
the King was then staying, for the purpose of receiving
his Majesty's commands in regard to the forces which
he had thus collected. His lordship's interview with
the King appears to have convinced his Majesty that
his efforts to serve him did not deserve the treatment
which he had received at the hands of the council.
The King desired him to hurry back to the forces
which he had collected, and to attack the town of
Manchester by assault. Obeying his majesty's instructions he returned to Lancashire, and joined his forces,
between four and five thousand in number, and having
completed every preparation for an attack upon Manchester, just about the time he was about to make it,
he received two despatches which interfered with the
carrying out of his intentions, and which must not
only have greatly discouraged him, but also have had
the effect of prejudicing the fortunes of the royal
cause. He was suddenly ordered to march, with
all his force, to Shrewsbury, in order to join the King's
army, which the Earl of Essex was there about to
attack, with a large number of men. The same day

which brought him the despatches just referred to, also conveyed to him the intelligence of his father's death, and his own elevation to the Earldom of Derby. To make matters still worse, and as if in order to add to the depression under which he must have been suffering by the two combined events to which we have adverted, the troops which he had collected were, on their arrival at Shrewsbury, placed under the command of others, whilst he himself was requested again to go into Lancashire in order to raise still further forces amongst a community which now looked upon the royal cause with a considerable amount of disfavour, even if it was not to a great extent actually hostile to it, in consequence of the manner in which the men already raised in that county by the Earl had been disposed.

Notwithstanding the disadvantageous position in which the royal cause was now placed in Lancashire, the Earl succeeded in taking the towns of Lancaster and Preston, commanding the troops in person. Having secured the two last named towns, he had made arrangements for an attack on Manchester, in accordance with the directions of the King, when the men under his command were again sent for to join his majesty's main army. Here was another disheartening exigency, calculated to dispirit the bravest or the most sanguine. But he was not thoroughly cast down. Seeing the necessities of his position, and that the cause of the King, in Lancashire, was now desperate, he determined to garrison Lathom House, and proceeded to do so. But his troubles and reverses were by no means at an end, for whilst engaged in the work of converting Lathom into a garrison, he was informed that the Isle of Man was about to be invaded by his enemies; and on receiving this intelligence, he at once determined on leaving England, for the purpose of defending and protecting his own kingdom of Man, leaving the defence of his mansion at Lathom, as well as the protection and keeping of his children to his noble and brave Countess, who, as will be seen from the sequel, displayed a heroism and devotion which has perhaps, scarcely a parallel in the history of ancient or modern times.

The fortifying and defence of Lathom House by his Countess, forms one of the most memorable events in "the great Stanley's" chequered career. Immediately on the Earl sailing for the Island, the Countess repaired to Lathom House for the purpose of superintending its fortification and defence. There can be no doubt that the opponents of the Earl, on his lordship leaving England, at once decided upon measures for crippling and harassing him in his absence, for he had scarcely left the shores of this country before the Countess was apprised of the intention of the leaders of the opposite forces to make an attack on the family mansion. With a vigour and resolution which characterized her entire conduct during the whole of this period, she adopted measures for making her position invulnerable. With this object, in addition to increasing the strength of her garrison, and augmenting her provisions and military stores, she adopted the wise and far-seeing precaution of taking under her protection and care, a considerable number of the middle and lower classes, upon whose devotion and loyalty she could rely ; and these parties so admitted into her confidence, formed a portion of her household, along with the servants of the family. Including these, and the troops in the service, which had been admitted within the garrison at Lathom, she had at her disposal a force of six regiments, having at the head of each a captain. These were selected from gentlemen of the county, who had volunteered to serve in the royal cause. They were, respectively, Captains Ogle, Chisenhall, Molyneux, Farington, Rawstorne, and Charnock; the command of the whole being entrusted to a brave officer, Major Farmer, a Scot. The Countess, and the officers in her confidence, had made these formidable preparations for the defence of the mansion, in so silent and reserved a manner that no one beyond its confines had the faintest notion that such a powerful force was ready to defend it. It was on the 28th of February, 1644, that the attacking party, headed by Fairfax, made their appearance, and when within a short distance from the mansion, Fairfax sent a trumpet, asking for a conference with the Countess, to which she consented ; but the record of the siege says that, in the meantime, " in order to make the best " show she could, she placed her inefficient and " unarmed men on the walls and tops of the towers, " and marshalled all the soldiers in good order, with " their respective officers, from the main guard in the " first court to the hall," and this having been effected, the interview took place. During the time it lasted, Fairfax offered her a removal to, and undisturbed residence at Knowsley, together with a moiety of the Earl's estate for the benefit of herself and family, if she would surrender the garrison. Her answer was as concise as it was significant. She said that " she was " under a double trust—faith to her husband and " allegiance to her sovereign ;" she added, that she desired a month to give her final reply, her object evidently being to communicate with the Earl, but Fairfax would not consent, on which the inflexible Countess said, " I hope, then, you will excuse me " if I preserve my honour and obedience, though, " perhaps, to my own ruin." The interview between the two having thus ended, and Fairfax having doubt-less satisfied himself that he had a truly noble and heroic opponent to deal with, took his departure, hesitating for some time as to whether he would lay siege to the place or take it by storm. He was made to believe, by a statement conveyed by a Mr. Rutter, one of the Earl's chaplains, to an officer of Fairfax's with whom he had a conversation, that the military force of the garrison was strong, but that they were short of provisions, and could not hold out for many days. Fairfax, on receiving this inaccurate intelligence, which, it should be stated, was purposely given, decided on not making an immediate assault, but on calling on the garrison to surrender, and at the expiration of a fortnight, in military terms demanded it. The reply of the Countess, prompt and conclusive, was as follows:— " I " have not yet forgotten what I owe to my Prince, and " to my Lord, and until I have lost my honour or my " life, I will defend this place."

In a few days after this interview the siege commenced, by Fairfax beginning to form trenches, when the Countess, who was in an elevated position, personally directing the defenders of the mansion, ordered a sally of two hundred men, when upwards of sixty of the enemy were killed, the Countess only losing two. Although the besiegers doubled their guard, and considerably withdrew their lines on meeting with this first disaster, the sallies from the defenders of the mansion were so continuous and effective, that upwards of three months had elapsed before their trenches were completed. Having effected this object, however, the large moat by which the house was surrounded was at length

approached, the besiegers then mounting a strong
battery besides an immense mortar. These formidable
preparations for attack having been made, the Countess
and her children were one day at dinner, when a shell
from this mortar fell into the very apartment in which
they were seated. A writer of the history of the seige
says, " the mortar piece was that which troubled us
" all. The little ladies had stomachs to digest cannon,
" but the stoutest soldiers had no hearts for grenadoes."
It was a providential circumstance that neither the
Countess nor any of the children were injured. It
was at this point in the siege that the Countess exhibited an amount of heroism and bravery unexampled,
perhaps, in the history of woman, if indeed, ever
equalled by man. No sooner had she recovered from
the surprise caused by this shell than the Countess
directed another sally, when some of the guns of
the enemy were spiked, whilst others were thrown
into the moat, with the exception of the mortar
which sent the shell, from the effects of which she
and her children escaped. This shell was secured
and triumphantly conveyed into the mansion. The
enemy now began to repair their works, in doing
which they were occupied for several days, but the
garrison, on successive occasions, destroyed them
again as soon as they were completed, the defence of
the mansion being most gallantly sustained. In the
engagements which took place at this time, between

the besiegers and the defenders of the mansion, upwards of one hundred of Fairfax's soldiers were killed, whilst their cannon were again spiked, the defenders losing only three men, with six or eight wounded. Prayer, by the defenders of the mansion, was offered up before every encounter, and thanks-givings invariably followed every success. In all or most of the engagements the Countess was present, directing the action of the troops, irrespective of her commander and officers, and the boldness which she displayed placed her in daily peril of her life.

Down to the present time the results had been clearly in favour of the defenders of the garrison, for the besiegers had already lost upwards of two thousand men. Whether or not Fairfax had lost all confidence in his commanding officer, by reason of the reverses which the attacking party had sustained, we cannot pretend to say, but certain it is that he removed him, and appointed in his stead one Colonel Rigby, a man who was deadly hostile to the Earl personally, and the circumstances in connection therewith were well known to the Countess. Rigby had not long been at the head of the assailants before he called upon the Countess, in coarse and insulting terms, to surrender. Her instant reply was no less withering than characteristic. On receiving the offensive summons, she at once called out, " Trumpet, "tell that insolent rebel Rigby, that if he presumes to

"send another summons within this place, I will
"have the messenger hanged up at the gates." The
condition of the besieged was, however, now becoming
daily worse, and one of much privation, for not only
was their ammunition almost exhausted by the
prolongation of the siege, but their corn and provisions
also were nearly all consumed. Such, indeed were
their necessities, that they had been reduced to the
extremity of having had to slaughter a considerable
number of their horses for food. But even, discourag-
ing as their prospects now looked, they did not allow
their spirits entirely to fall, as will be seen from the
following extract from a description of the siege,
written in the interest of the besieged:—" Now neither
"ditches nor aught else troubled our soldiers, their
"grand terror, the mortar piece, which had frightened
"them from their meat and sleep, lying like a dead
"lion, quietly among them; every one had his eye and
"his foot upon it, shouting and rejoicing as merrily as
"they used to do with their ale and bagpipes. . . .
"Mr. Rigby's spirit being laid within our circle, we
"were scarcely sensible of a siege, except by the
"restraint upon our liberty. But our men continually
"vexed their quiet, either by the excursion of a few in
"the night, or by frequent alarms which the captains
"gave the soldiers leave to invent and exercise for
"their recreation. Sometimes, in spite of their perdues,
"they would steal a cord round some tree near the

"enemy's works, and, bringing the end round, would
"make it terrible with many ranks and files of light
"matches ; sometimes dogs, and once a forlorn horse,
"handsomely starred with matches, being turned out of
"the gate, appeared in the dark night like some huge
"constellation!" Rigby ultimately raised the siege,
after the disastrous losses which he had sustained, on
the 27th of May, 1644, under the following circumstances. The Earl having heard of the straits to which
his Countess and her followers had been reduced, by the
prolongation of the attack, came over from the Isle of
Man, with the view of obtaining further assistance
for the continued defence of Lathom. This assistance
was extended to him by Prince Rupert; and Rigby,
on hearing of it fled with his troops to Bolton.
Thus was brought to a close, the first attack on Lathom
House, which for a period of three months was
defended by a brave and noble hearted woman, in a
manner which will hand down her name to all
posterity as one of the most devoted, large hearted,
and heroic of her sex.

Rigby and his army of besiegers having thus
withdrawn themselves from Lathom, and taken
possession of Bolton, the Earl followed Prince Rupert,
who, with a large army, was before the last-named
town, "being," we are told, "truly happy of an
"occasion to fight with the merciless besiegers of
"a princess in misery, and forthwith, with all

"gallantry and resolution led on his men to an assault."
The siege of Bolton took place on the 28th of May,
1644, and on the Earl of Derby arriving at the scene
of action, he desired Prince Rupert to place two
companies under his command, expressing his fears
that the town would be again besieged if the Prince, ·
with his army, left. The Prince was at first disinclined
to comply with the Earl's request, in consequence of
the hazardous nature of the undertaking proposed by
him ; but the latter pressed it, stating that he would
lead the van, and that "he would either enter the
the town or leave his body in the ditch." Prince
Rupert ultimately complied with the Earl's wishes,
and the latter, with 200 men, marched to the walls,
and after a quarter of an hour's desperate fighting,
took the town, the Earl being at the head of his men,
and the first to enter. Rigby himself made a precipitate retreat, leaving 2000 men behind him, most
of whom were slain. All the colours taken were
sent to Lathom House, where they remained, as
trophies of victory, up to the time when the vener-
able mansion was destroyed by the rebels. One of
the historians of the siege says that "the Earl
"of Derby desiring to be one of the first avengers
"of that barbarity and cruelty displayed to his
"lady, with a part of the prince's own horse,
"charged a troop of the enemy, which had bravely
"issued out of the town to disorder and vex our

"fort in the assault. These he chased to the very
"walls, where he slew the cornet, and with his own
"hand took the colours, being the first ensign taken
"that day, and which he sent to his highness."

We must here digress a little for the purpose of
showing the ultimate rate and disposal of Lathom.
We have just spoken of the first attack or siege.
After this siege it appears that Lathom House was
placed in charge of Colonel Rawstorne, who supplied
the garrison with provisions and ammunition for
sustaining another siege. In July, 1645, the siege
was renewed by General Egerton, who had 4000
soldiers under his command. The General fixed
upon Ormskirk as his head quarters. For a time the
garrison resisted the besiegers, but at length, having
no further ammunition, and, what was still worse,
being disappointed in the expectation of a reinforce-
ment from the king, who was then at Chester, the
commander, we are told, was obliged to surrender
Lathom House into the hands of the Parliamentary
forces, " upon bare terms of mercy." At the time of
the surrender, the mansion contained twelve pieces
of ordnance, besides a large store of arms and ammunition.

The besiegers soon converted the most valuable
effects of the house into booty; the rich silk hangings
of the beds were rent in pieces; the towers from which
so many fatal shots had proceeded were demolished,

and the sun of Lathom seemed for ever to have set. The following somewhat amusing account of the surrender appears in a newspaper of the time, called the "Perfect Diurnal." In its publication of December 8, 1645, this paper says:—"On Saturday, "December 6, after the house was up, there came "letters to the speaker of the Commons' House, of "the surrender of Lathom House in Lancashire, be- "longing to the Earl of Derby, which his lady, the "Countess of Derby, proving herself the better soldier "of the two, hath above these two years kept in "opposition to our forces." We may here state under what circumstances Lathom House became the property of its present possessors. At the time of the Restoration it again became the property of the Earl of Derby, but it had then been almost demolished, and the family resided at Knowsley. It was the intention of the ninth Earl, William Richard George, to have re-built it, and he had commenced the work, but died before its completion. At the time of his death, however, he had erected what composes a part of the south front of the present house. On the Earl's death it became the property of his eldest daughter, Henrietta, who was twice married, first to the Earl of Anglesey, and secondly to Lord Ashburnham. The last-named nobleman disposed of it to Henry Furnese, Esq., who again sold it, in the year 1724, to Sir Thomas Bootle. Knight, of

Melling, in Lancashire. Subsequently, Sir Thomas's neice and heiress was married to Richard Wilbraham, Esq., of Rode Hall, in Cheshire, and by this marriage it came into the possession of the Skelmersdale family, the first Lord Skelmersdale being the eldest son of the marriage. It is not a little remarkable that through marriage, Lathom House is again associated with the Derby family, the present Countess of Derby, who was the Hon. Miss Wilbraham, being a daughter of the first Lord Skelmersdale. We read that during the time of those historic periods, when it was the residence of the Earls of Derby, Lathom House, "for magnificence and hospitality, surpassed all the "residences of the north, assuming, in those respects, "the attitude of a royal court, and its possessions "were regarded with such veneration and esteem, "that the following harmless inversion was 'familiar as "household words': 'God save the Earl of Derby and "the King.'"

We now, after this digression, return to our narrative. After the raising of the siege of Lathom, the Earl, accompanied by his Countess, returned to the Isle of Man, followed by a considerable number of royalists of England, who, "wearied with being "so often awakened at midnight with the King's "and Parliament's troops, both equally feared, because "equally plundering," quitted their native country, in order to pass life in quiet and retirement along with the Earl. "Some too," we are told, "who had "served with the Earl in his battles, and been invalided "through wounds, betook themselves with him, to this "sanitorium." Amongst them was Captain Edward Halsall, wounded in the siege of Lathom House, of which he has left an account; and Major Blundell, of Crosby, whose thigh had been shattered by a musket ball on the taking of Lancaster. Fairfax, shortly after this period, behaved in a disgracefully treacherous manner to the Earl, who was anxious to have his children sent to England for their education. Fairfax had given the Earl an assurance that his children should be safe; but, notwithstanding this promise, they were seized, whilst travelling in England, by an order of the House of Commons, and confined as prisoners in Liverpool. During the time his children were so detained, the Parliament, through Fairfax, tempted him to forsake the cause of his royal master, by giving up possession of the Isle of Man, offering, if he would do so, to restore to him his children, as well as the whole of his estates, but they could not shake his loyalty and devotion to the King, for he firmly replied "That he was greatly afflicted at the sufferings "and miseries of his children; that it was not in the "nature of great and noble minds to punish innocent "children for the offences of their parents; that it "would be a clemency in Sir Thomas Fairfax either

"to send them back to him, or to their mother's
"friends in France and Holland; but if he would do
"neither, his children must submit to the mercy of
"Almighty God, but should never be released by his
"disloyalty." His devotion to the King was resented,
on the part of Parliament, by the sequestration of his
estates, and the continued imprisonment of his children.
The attempt to shake his loyalty was on more than
one occasion renewed, and after the execution of the
King, the Parliament endeavoured to weaken the
allegiance of the Manx people towards the Earl, and,
as more than one historian says, even went so far as
to plot against the lives of the Earl and his family.
Charles the Second was then an exile in France,
but the Earl acknowledged no authority over him—
recognised no one but Charles as his sovereign.
At length, in June, 1649, the Parliament, through
General Ireton, again offered to restore all his English
estates, together with his children, if he would
surrender his right and sovereignty of the Isle of Man,
when he again indignantly refused to entertain the
proposal, and sent Ireton the following reply:—

    "Castletown, Isle of Man, 12th July, 1649.

    "Sir—I received your letter with indignation, and
"with scorn return you this answer; that I cannot but
"wonder where you should gather any hopes from me
"that I should, like you, prove treacherous to my
"sovereign, since you cannot but be sensible of

" my former actings in his late Majesty's service, from
" which principle of loyalty I am in no whit separated.
" I scorn your proffers, disdain your favor, and abhor
" your treason ; and am so far from delivering up this
" Island to your advantage, that I will keep it, to the
" utmost of my power, to your destruction. Take this
" for your final answer, and forbear any further solici-
" tation, for if you trouble me with any more messages
" on this occasion, I will burn the paper and hang the
" bearer.   This is the immutable resolution, and shall
" be the undoubted practice of him who accounts it his
" chiefest glory to be,

> " His Majesty's most loyal and obedient servant,
>
> " DERBY."

During the stay of the Earl and his Countess in the
Isle of Man, after leaving England on the siege of
Lathom being raised, he kept up a series of brilliant
courts at Rushen Castle, where he, to a great extent,
resided, and at Christmas, 1644, he held a splendid
festival or carnival, which is thus graphically
described :—" The right honourable James, Earl of
" Derby, and his right honourable Countess, on the
" last day in Christmas, invited all the Officers,
" spiritual and temporal, the Clergy, the twenty-four
" Keys of the Isle, the Coroners, with all their wives,
" and likewise the best sort of the inhabitants of the
" Isle ; when the right honourable Charles, Lord
" Strange, with his train, the right honourable Ladies

" with their attendants, were most gloriously decked
" with silver and gold broidered works, and most costly
" ornaments, bracelets on their hands, chains on their
" necks, jewels on their foreheads, ear-rings in their
" ears, and crowns on their heads. And after the mask
" to a feast, which was most royal and plentiful, with
" shooting of ordnance." It appears that at this
pageant, the Countess was the " cynosure of all
observers," and elicited the warmest admiration of the
assembled guests, who were eulogistic of her brave and
heroic deeds and valour in the defence of Lathom
House. Whilst the Earl was now residing in his
territory of the Isle of Man, it was suspected that there
were several parties in the island, who were secretly
plotting against the Earl, and in league with the
Parliamentary agents in England. Amongst the
persons so suspected were William and Edward
Christian, who held an influential position in the
island, and for several years past had professed
the warmest attachment to the Earl and his family.
It is supposed that the Earl had a strong belief, from
circumstances which had come to his knowledge, that
the Christians were disaffected towards him, but his
lordship did not allow his suspicions to be generally
known, nor did he in any way so deport himself
towards the Christians as to induce the latter to believe
that treachery was imputed to them; but the following
extracts from his lordship's own remarks and observa-

tions, in reference to those present at the Christmas carnival, show that he was a close judge of character, and could readily distinguish the difference between a real and a feigned homage offered to him. The Christians were present at the festival, and in speaking of the company the Earl significantly and satirically remarks, " I observed much the counten- " ances of those who bid me welcome, and the eyes are " often glass windows through which you may see the " heart; and although I will not presently censure by " the look, yet will I neither neglect some judgment " thereof; so it is that your eyes must be ever open to " see each other's eyes, their countenances and actions ; " your ears must listen to all what is said, even what " is whispered. For to this end, God has given us two " eyes and two ears. So also you have but one tongue, " to the end you speak not much, for speaking much " you are sure to say something vain. I never knew " a prattler without repentance." From this extract it is tolerably obvious that the Earl must have been more than ordinarily observant of his guests on the night of the festival, which the circumstances of the times, in connection with what afterwards took place in the island, amply justified. We may here state that his lordship's suspicions, at this period, are supposed to have been directed towards Captain Edward Christian, who, after professing the greatest attachment to the Earl, when he (Christian) first took up his residence in the island, was subsequently found plotting the ruin and downfall of his lordship, and was in close league with the Covenanters and Roundheads who came over to the island from England and Scotland, for the purpose of spreading sedition among the Earl's retainers and friends. There can be no doubt that the Earl had a formidable array of enemies in the island, more particularly among the Puritans, who condemned the Christmas festival, as will be seen from the following characteristic description of their feelings and opinions :—

"The more puritanically disposed expressed "themselves as shocked at the pomp and pride of the "Earl and his family, the vain earthly show by which "they were surrounded, the levity of the conversation, "the prodigality and wealth of the feast, which might "have supplied the wants of so many families of the "poor peasants scattered over the mountains and "heaths of the Isle of Man. Well might the Earl, "they said, seek to rob the people of the rights of "their ancient treasures, in order to get heavier rents "to support so much extravagance. But a day was "coming, when the groans of the oppressed would "go up to heaven, and bring down judgment on the "pride of Derby and all the malignants associated "with him, in his ungodly revels. And what would "the priests of Baal do when their idol was cast down, "and righteousness exalted in the land ? Those

" worldly-minded pastors, who had neglected their flocks
" scattered in the wilderness, to come and join them-
" selves in rioting and drunkenness with the servants
" of Mammon, the profane followers of that Popish
" Countess, who kept Jesuits in her house, and had
" dared to defy the armies of the Lord, under that
" godly man, Rigby, and had slain the supporters of the
" Solemn League and Covenant."

The Earl and his family continued to reside in
the Isle of Man for several years longer, but it is
quite clear that he never ceased to entertain the hope
and desire to overthrow the Parliament, and restore
Charles the Second to the throne. In the year 1648, it
was obvious that a project was entertained by the
Parliament to seize upon the King, and in order to
take part in the struggle on the side of his majesty
and the Royalists, the Earl made arrangements to
leave the island for England. He had during his
residence in the island, taken a lively interest in its
social and political condition, and the well-being of
those around him; and although there had on several
occasions been manifestations of discontent in several
quarters on the ground of alleged undue imposts
levied by the Earl on the inhabitants, it is abundantly
clear that he was always anxious to redress their
grievances, and the following letter shows the good
feeling which existed between the Earl and his Manx
subjects:—

"Oct. 28th, 1648.

"Sir,—I am not very sure whether I can be at
"the next Head Court at Castletown, but, however, I
"think good to advertise you of my desire, which is by
"your mouth, to thank my officers and the twenty-four
"keys for that free gift in money which they so readily
"bestowed on me in my late intended journey to
"England; that failing, I have (as all know) returned
"back the money, which, though I was willing to part
"with all, yet shall I never part with the remembrance
"of that love from which it came, and I heartily rejoice
"that thereby I find myself so well seated in the
"affections of this people, whose good and profit, I take
"God to witness, I shall ever study to advance.

"I am, therefore, upon these considerations, en-
"couraged to let them know my present occasion in
"these necessitous times; for the supply of which I
"would by no means keep that which was given me,
"but would rather choose to try the same affections
"once again, in the way of a loan, the sum of five
"hundred pounds, which I do hereby faithfully promise
"to repay, so soon as it shall please God to restore me
"to my estate in England; and I trust that by my
"return of the same affection back again unto them.
"whenever I shall have occasion to express it, they shall
"find they have laid up their money in a good hand, to
"receive it again with many other advantages. This I

" do desire you, together with my love, to recommend
" unto them, and so I rest.

" Your very loving friend,
" J. DERBY.

" From Bishop's Court,
" For the Governor of Castletown, there."

The intention, however, to seize the King, was not
carried out, and the Earl remained in the Isle of Man
until the year 1651. It was in January of that year,
that Charles the Second was crowned at Scone,
swearing to observe the Solemn League and Covenant.
In April following he was at the head of an army in
Scotland. During the summer he advanced into
England, and in the month of August he arrived at
Warrington, heading a numerous body of forces, which
consisted of 14,000 men. Thence he proceeded through
Cheshire and Shropshire, to Worcester, where, on the
22nd of August, he was proclaimed King. He then invited the English Royalists to aid and support him with
all the forces they could raise, and, amongst others, he
summoned the Earl of Derby, who at once left the
Isle of Man to join his sovereign, leaving his Countess
and three of his children in the care of Illiam Dhone,
the Receiver-General of the Island. He took with
him, from the island, a force of 300 Royalists, including his favourite governor, John Greenalgh, who
was accounted a bold and daring soldier in the field.

On the arrival of the Earl in England he had a conference with Major-General Massey, at Warrington,
the King, who had gone south, having left the major
to receive and confer with his lordship. On meeting
Major General Massey, the Earl was somewhat astonished at the demand made upon him by the major.
The latter had brought with him a number of Presbyterian ministers, who, to the surprise and disgust of
his lordship, called upon him not only to swear allegiance to the Solemn League and Covenant, but likewise demanded that he should "dismiss all the Papists
whom he had brought over with him." The Earl,
being by no means disposed to submit to the conditions
thus sought to be imposed upon him, replied that "on
" these terms he might long since have been restored to
" his whole estate, and that blessed martyr Charles the
" First to all his kingdom—that he came not to dispute
" on religion, but to fight for his Majesty's Restoration."
But the Presbyterian ministers insisted on their
terms being complied with, when the Earl exclaimed,
" If I perish, I perish, but if my master suffer, the
" blood of another prince and all the ensuing miseries
" of the nation will lie at your doors." The Earl then
proceeded to Preston, having only 800 troops in all,
including the 300 which he had brought over with him
from the Isle of Man. With this weak force he
advanced, on the 25th of August, to Wigan, with the
intention of taking up his quarters there. Here,

however, he was unexpectedly attacked the next day, by Colonel Lilburn, who was at the head of an overwhelming force of 3000 horse and foot, 1800 being dragoons, whom Cromwell had sent to hang upon the King's rear. This was the occasion of the well-known battle of Wigan Lane. It will easily be believed that in this fearfully unequal conflict the Earl and his little army were worsted, but notwithstanding the immense odds against him, he fought for two hours, performing prodigies of valour, and receiving, in this sanguinary engagement, seven shots in his breastplate, thirteen cuts in his beaver, five or six wounds on his arms and shoulders, and had two horses killed under him. It is little less than miraculous, that twice he dashed through the whole body of the enemy, and on making a third attempt, was overwhelmed with numbers, several of the officers of his force, including Lord Witherington, Sir Thomas Tyldesley, and other gentlemen being killed. The Earl, having succeeded in mounting a third horse, fought his way through the ranks of the enemy, in company with his faithful Governor Greenalgh, and five other officers. One of the historians of the battle of Wigan Lane, says, describing his lordship's escape, that "in this third charge, upon the fall of "Lord Witherington, his lordship mounted his horse, "and being seconded by six gentlemen of the party, he, "with them, fought his way through a great body of

"the enemy, into the town; where his lordship, quit-
"ting his horse, leapt in at a door, that stood open,
"and, suddenly shutting it before the enemy could
"reach it, the woman of the house* kept it shut so
"long till his lordship was conveyed to a place of
"privacy, where he lay concealed for many hours,
"notwithstanding the most industrious search of
"the enemy." Having at length made his escape,
he passed through Shropshire and Staffordshire, to
Boscobel House, and finally reached the King at
Worcester, where he joined his Majesty in time to
take part in the fatal battle of Worcester, which was
fought on the 3rd of September, only eight days
after the deadly engagement at Wigan, his wounds
yet bleeding and green. At the close of this battle,
he conducted the King with great skill and secresy,
through St. Martin's Gate to the celebrated retreats
of Whiteladies and Boscobel, where he himself had
stayed only the day before, on his way to the battle.
This was the last time he ever saw his Majesty, for
fate had decreed that in a few short weeks afterwards
the loyal and devoted Earl's life was to be sacrificed
on the scaffold. On taking leave of the King, accom-

---

* This house was then, and for several years afterwards, "The
Dog" public house, in which there was a brass plate with the arms
of Man upon it, round which was the inscription "Honi soit qui mal
y pense," with an intimation that that was the house into which
Lord Derby fled, and that the room in which his lordship was concealed, was afterwards called "Beeston Castle."

panied by from forty to fifty of his followers, he was returning with all possible speed to his own county, when, just as he entered Cheshire, he was attacked by a regiment of foot and a troop of horse, under the command of Major Edge, to whom he surrendered on a promise of quarter for life; but these terms of surrender were most infamously violated, at the immediate instance, as was subsequently proved, of Bradshaw, Rigby, and Birch, who were notoriously three of the Earl's bitterest personal enemies. These three having represented to Cromwell, that the well-being and peace of the Commonwealth rendered it unsafe for the Earl to be allowed to live, the Parliament sent down a commission to nineteen persons in Cheshire, to try the Earl on a charge of high treason. This commission was composed of five Colonels, three Lieutenant-Colonels, and eleven Captains, all well known to be hostile to Derby, and the "trial" may simply be pronounced a mockery. In vain did the Earl urge the "quarter for life" extended to him by Major Edge, on his surrender, as a reason against his being *tried* for life. He was condemned to death, and directed to be executed in four days, in his own town of Bolton, the latter portion of the sentence more especially showing the heartless and wicked animus by which his judges were actuated. After sentence had been passed, the Earl's son, Charles, repaired to London with all possible speed, in order to

lay his father's case before Parliament, and to petition
for a delay in carrying out the sentence, but Cromwell, by an act which will for ever remain as
an indelible blot on his character and memory, prevented the application from being successful. The
facts having been laid before the House, Cromwell
saw that a majority of the members were inclined to
vote for the execution being, at least, delayed, and on
the Speaker putting the question he resorted to the
questionable expedient of leaving the House, accompanied by eight or nine members whom he had
induced to follow him, and by this discreditable
proceeding reduced the number of members present
to under forty. The House being thus counted out, the
praiseworthy efforts of Lord Strange to save his
father's life failed. An occurrence, however, took
place on the day of his trial which nearly resulted in
his persecutors being baffled in their deadly and
murderous intentions. On the night of Saturday,
October 11th, he managed to get on to the leads of
the tower in which he was confined in Chester Castle.
Whilst he was on the top of these leads, a rope was
thrown up to him from the exterior of the Castle, and
having succeeded in securing it, he descended in
safety, and made his way to the banks of the Dee,
where a boat was in readiness to take him away, but
here he was again tracked by the officers in charge,
and conveyed back to the Castle, where he remained

until Tuesday, the 14th, the day before his execution, when he was taken to Leigh, and from that town to Bolton. Just before he left Chester Castle for Leigh, on the 14th of October, two of his daughters, Lady Catherine and Lady Amelia, who had been staying in Chester, had their last interview with him. Whilst he was in Chester Castle, after his condemnation, he wrote two beautiful letters to his wife, and one to his children in the Isle of Man. These letters were entrusted to the Rev. Humphrey Bagaley, who was permitted to attend him to the last, and who has written a touching narrative of the last hours of his life. His letters to his family, and his last utterances on the scaffold, "display," says Lodge, "one of the "purest examples extant of the courage of a soldier, "the patience of a philosopher, and the piety of a "Christian." The following is the letter written to his Countess, on Sunday the 12th, the day after his trial, and perhaps a more truly affectionate communication was never penned :—

"My Dear Heart,—I have heretofore sent you "comfortable lines, but alas, I have now no word of "comfort saving to our last and best refuge, which is "Almighty God, to whose will we must submit; and "when we consider how he hath disposed of these "nations, and the government thereof, we have no "more to do than lay our hands upon our mouths, "judging ourselves and acknowledging our sins, joined

"with others to have been the cause of these miseries,
"and to call on him with tears for mercy. The
"Governor of this place, Colonel Duckenfield, is General
"of the forces which are now going against the Isle
"of Man; and however you might do for the present,
"in time it would be a grievous and troublesome thing
"to resist, especially those that at this hour command
"the three nations; wherefore, my advice, notwith-
"standing my great affection to that place, is that
"you would make conditions for yourself, and children,
"and servants, and people there, and such as came
"over with me, to the end you may get to some place
"of rest, where you may not be concerned in war, and,
"taking thought of your poor children, you may in
"some sort provide for them: then prepare yourself
"to come to your friends above, in that blessed place
"where bliss is, and no mingling of opinion. I
"conjure you, my dearest heart, by all those graces
"that God hath given you, that you exercise your
"patience in this great and strange trial. If harm
"come to you, then I am dead indeed; and until then
"I shall live in you, who are truly the best part of
"myself. When there is no such thing as I, in being,
"then look upon yourself and my poor children; then
"take comfort, and God will bless you. I acknowledge
"the great goodness of God to have given me such a
"wife as you—so great an honour to my family—so
"excellent a companion to me—so pious—so much of

" all that can be said of good, I must confess it impos-
" sible to say enough thereof.   I ask God pardon with
" all my soul that I have not been enough thankful
" for so great a benefit; and when I have done any-
" thing at any time that might justly offend you, with
" joined hands I also ask you pardon.   I have no
" more to say to you at this time than my prayers for
" the Almighty blessing to you, my dear Mall, and
" Ned, and Billy (his children).   Amen; sweet Jesus!"

He also wrote her another letter, couched in the
same affectionate language as the foregoing, and again
alluding to her position in the island.   This letter
concludes as follows :—

"You know how much that place (the Isle of
" Man) is my darling; but, since it is God's will to
" dispose, in the manner it is, of this nation, and
" Ireland too, there is nothing further to be said of the
" Isle of Man, but to refer all to the will of God, and
" to procure the best conditions you can for yourself
" and our poor family and friends there, and those
" that came over with me; and so trusting in the
" assistance and goodness of God, begin the world
" again, though near winter, whose cold and piercing
" blasts are much more tolerable than the malicious
" approaches of a poisoned serpent, or an inveterate and
" malign enemy, from whose powers the Lord of Heaven
" bless and preserve you; God Almighty comfort you
" and my poor children; and the Son of God, whose blood

"was shed for our good, preserve your lives, that by
"the good will and mercy of God we may meet once
"more upon earth, and last in the kingdom of heaven,
"where we shall be for ever free from all rapine,
"plunder, and violence; and so I rest everlastingly,
"Your most faithful,
"DERBY."

And in his letter to his children, he enjoins them
to obey their mother with all cheerfulness, and not
to grieve her, adding "for she is your example, your
"nursery, your counsellor, your all under God; there
"never was, nor never can be, a more deserving person."

The day appointed for his execution, the 15th of
October, his lordship arrived at Bolton, about mid-
day, from Leigh, guarded by a millitary escort, consisting of two troops of cavalry, and a company of
infantry. Intense sympathy was shewn towards his
lordship, and it is scarcely too much to say that the
whole town was in tears. Having alighted, he was
taken to a house near the market cross, and accompanied by his friends and servants, he went into it, remaining there until three o'clock in the afternoon, the
time being occupied, to a great extent, in prayer, and in
conversation as to the manner in which he had lived,
and how he had prepared to die. "The fear of death
"was no trouble to him, and his only care was for his
"wife and children; but he was satisfied to commit

"them to God." Soon after three o'clock he was attended to the scaffold, when he proceeded to deliver a lengthened address, which he had committed to writing, and which was as follows:—

"I come, and am content to die in this town, "where I endeavoured to come the last time I was in "Lancashire, and to a place where I persuaded myself "to be welcome, in regard the people thereof have "reason to be satisfied in my love and affection to "them; and that now they understand sufficiently. I "am no man of blood, as some have falsely slandered "me, especially in the killing of a captain in this "town; whose death is now declared on oath, so as "the time and place now appears under the hand of a "master in chancery, besides the several attestations "of a gentleman of honour in the kingdom, who was "in the fight in this town, and of others of good "report, both in the town and country; and I am "confident that there are some in this place who can "witness my mercy and care, for sparing many men's "lives that day.

"As for my crime, (as some are pleased to call it,) 'to come into this country with the King. I hope it "deserves a better name; for I did it in obedience "to his call, whom I hold myself obliged to obey, "according to the protestation I took in Parliament, in "his father's time. I confess I love monarchy, and "I love my master, Charles, the second of that name,

" whom I myself proclaimed in this country to be
" King. The Lord bless him and preserve him; I
" assure you he is the most goodly, virtuous, valiant,
" and most discreet King that I know lives this day;
" and I wish so much happiness to this people after
" my death, that he may enjoy *his* right, and then
" they cannot want *their* rights. I profess here in the
" presence of God, I always fought for peace and I
" had no other reason, for I wanted neither means nor
" honours, nor did I seek to enlarge either. By my
" King's predecessors mine were raised to a high con-
" dition, it is well known to the country; and it is as
" well known that by his enemies I am condemned to
" suffer by new and unknown laws. The Lord send
" us our King again, and our old laws again, and the
" Lord send us our religion again.

"As for that which is practised now, it has no
" name; and methinks there is more talk of religion
" than any good effects of it.

"Truly, to me it seems I die for God, the King,
" and the laws, and this makes me not ashamed of my
" life, nor afraid of my death."

When his lordship made use of the words "the
" King and the laws," a trooper cried "We have no
" King, and we will have no lords." A fear of mutiny
amongst the soldiers caused his lordship to be inter-
rupted, at which some of the officers were troubled,
and his friends much grieved, his lordship having

6

freedom of speech promised him. His lordship seeing
the troopers scattered in the streets, cutting and
slashing the people with their swords, said "What's
"the matter, gentlemen? Where's the guilt? I fly
"not, and here is none to pursue you?" He then
handed the paper to his servant, desiring him to let
the world know the contents of the latter part of his
intended speech, which were as follow :—

"My sentence (upon which I am brought hither),
"was by a Council of War; nothing in the captain's
"case alleged against me; which Council, I had reason
"to expect, would have justified my plea for quarter,
"that being an ancient and honourable plea amongst
"soldiers, and not violated (that I know of) till this
"time that I am made the first suffering precedent, in
"this case. I wish no other to suffer in the like case.
"Now I must die, and am ready to die, I thank my
"God, with a good conscience, without any malice,
"on any ground whatever: though others would not
"find mercy upon me, upon just and fair grounds :
"so my Saviour prayed for His enemies, and so do I
"for mine."

"As for my faith, and my religion, thus much I
"have at this time to say: I profess my faith to be in
"Jesus Christ, who died for me, from whom I look
"for my salvation; that is, through His only merits
"and sufferings; and I die a dutiful son of the
"Church of England, as it was established in my late

"master's time and reign, and is yet professed in the
"Isle of Man, which is no little comfort to me."

"I thank my God for the quiet of my conscience
"at this time, and the assurance of those joys that
"are prepared for those that fear Him.   Good people,
"pray for me: I do for you.   The God of Heaven
"bless you all, and send you peace; that God, that is
"truth itself, give you grace, peace, and truth. Amen."

A few moments before the execution took place,
he desired that the block might be removed, so as
to face the Church, and his request having been
complied with, he said "I will look towards Thy
"sanctuary while I am here, as I hope to live in Thy
"heavenly sanctuary for ever hereafter."   He then laid
his head upon the block, and stretching out his arms,
said, "Blessed be God's glorious name for ever and
"ever.   Amen.   Let the whole earth be filled with
"His glory."   He then lifted up his hands as a
signal for the executioner, but, apparently, not under-
standing the Earl's movement, he did not strike the
blow; on which his lordship rose, and addressing
him, said, "What have I done that I die not?   Well,
"I will lay myself down once again in peace, and I
"hope I shall enjoy everlasting peace;" and then
adding, in a loud tone. "The Lord bless my wife and
"children, and the Lord bless us all," he again gave
the signal, when one blow from the headsman
sufficed for his decapitation, and the great Stanley

was sacrificed for devotion to his King, amidst the tears and sobs of a sympathising multitude.

There is considerable diversity of opinion amongst historians, as to the time and circumstances under which the body was conveyed from Bolton to be buried. One authority says, " On the following day, the re- " mains of his lordship were conveyed from Bolton " to Ormskirk, to be interred in the family vault of " the house of Stanley," whilst the author of " A " Discourse of the War in Lancashire," says, " with " his clothes upon him, he was put into the coffin " there readie, which had abundance of seeds in it, to " receive the bloode, and he was carried away that " night, to Wiggan, and from there to Ormskirke, to " be buried amongst his ancestors." Seacome, on the other hand says, " his body was then taken up and " *stript*, as he had directed, and laid in his coffin." When the body was put into the coffin to be carried to Ormskirk, the following lines, by an unknown hand, were thrown into it :—

" Wit, bounty, courage, three here in one lie dead ;
" A Stanley's hand, Vere's heart, and Cecil's head."

The deceased Earl had, by his Countess, Charles, his successor, besides two younger sons, who died in infancy. He had also four daughters, one of whom died young, the others being married to William Wentworth, second Earl of Stafford; Henry Pierre-

pont, Marquis of Dorchester; and John, Marquis of
Athol. By this last marriage the Barony of Strange,
by writ 1628, and the lordship of Man, were even-
tually carried to James, Second Duke of Athol.

As regards the unfortunate Countess, there are
again several conflicting statements respecting her condition and fate; but it is admitted that Colonels Birch
and Duckinfield, soon after the death of her husband,
attacked the Isle of Man, when through the imputed
treachery of William Christian—whom the Earl had
cherished from his childhood, and to whom, at his
final departure, he had committed the care of his
lady and their offspring, as well as the command of
the infantry of the island—the Countess and her
children were betrayed into the hands of their enemies. Seacome, in confirmation of this says:—
"Christian (Illiam Dhone) having prepared the coun-
"try for the execution of his treachery, suffered the
"Parliamentary forces to land without resistance, seized
"upon the lady and her children, with the Governors
"of both castles, and the next morning brought them
"prisoners to Duckinfield and Birch, who told Duckin-
"field that her ladyship had surrendered the island
"upon articles. She requested of Colonels Duckinfield
"and Birch, but especially of Christian, who had
"formed and acquiesced to those articles, that she and
"her children might have leave to retire to Peel
"Castle, from whence she proposed that she might in

"some little time, get over to her friends in France or
" Holland, or some place of rest or refuge, but she was
" utterly denied that favour by her hard-hearted and
" inhuman enemies. She and her children continued
" prisoners in the island until his Majesty's happy
" Restoration, (enduring all their sufferings with a
" generous resolution and Christian patience) and
" then, expecting justice against her lord's murderers,
" her son restored to the sequestered estates of her
" father, and some compensation for the immense losses
" and devastations of her family; but failing of all,
" her great heart over-filled with grief and endless
" sorrow, burst in pieces, and she died at Knowsley
" House, with that Christian temper and exemplary
" piety in which she had always lived."

It is only right to say that the accuracy of the
above statement is denied, more particularly as to
her alleged imprisonment in the Isle of Man, until
after the Restoration, and in support of this, it is
said that on the 7th of August, 1656, being then
resident at Knowsley, she presented the Rev.
Nathaniel Heywood to the Vicarage of Ormskirk ; and
Cumming, in his recent interesting work, " The Great
Stanley," states that the original of the presentation is
still in the possession of a member of the family.   He
adds that " On the 26th of February, 1660, being 'the
" 'true and undoubted patron,' she nominated the Rev.
" John Greenalgh, S.T.B., to the Rectory of Bury, having

"procured the resignation of the Rev. John Lightfoot,
"the last incumbent." He then observes: "These do
"not look like the acts of a poor prisoner, confined, as it
"is said, in a dark dungeon of Rushen Castle, with two
"of her children, who are stated to have there caught
"the small-pox,—and at the end of the time permitted
"to walk about the Isle of Man destitute, and sub-
"sisting on alms. Can we believe that her son,
"Charles, who during that time was, undoubtedly,
"living free, and in the enjoyment of a competency,
"would have been so wanting in filial affection as to
"allow his mother to be in absolute want, and suf-
"fering such indignities? Unfortunately, the posi-
"tive evidences as to the residence of the Countess
"between 1652 and 1660 are still wanting, but the
"negative evidence is certainly very strong, against
"the unsupported testimony of Seacome." The pre-
cise date of her death, however, is not in dispute.
She died at Knowsley, on the 21st of March, 1663,
aged 57, and was buried on the 6th of April, by the
side of her husband, in the family vault at Ormskirk.

CHAPTER V.

CHARLES, EIGHTH EARL, TO EDWARD, ELEVENTH EARL OF DERBY.

THE great Stanley was succeeded by his son Charles, Lord Strange, as eighth Earl of Derby; but for many years it was only an empty title, as the part which his father took in the Civil War, on behalf of the King, had sadly impoverished the family. Charles married Dorothea Helena, daugher of John Kirkhoven, Baron of Rupa, in Holland. By this marriage he had four sons and two daughters. For several years after his father's execution, and until the period of the Restoration, he was in needy circumstances, if not in actual pecuniary distress, and lived along with his mother and family in economical retirement at Bidston Hall, in Cheshire, for Lathom House was a heap of ruins, and Knowsley in a condition little superior. Besides this, more than one-half of the estates of the family were either sold or sequestered; he possessed not one in Lancashire, Cheshire, Westmorland, Cumberland, Warwickshire, York, or Wales, from which he could not see others of equal or greater value, that had been lost by his father for his devotion to the cause of Charles the First.   And yet, when a bill to effect the redemption of his estates had unanimously passed both Houses of Parliament, the royal assent was withheld by the son of that King, for whom the illustrious Earl had ruined the fortunes of his family, and laid his own head upon the block. Two years before the Restoration, the Earl took a part in resisting the conduct of Parliament, which led to his imprisonment. Cromwell dying in 1658, was succeeded in the Commonwealth, but really in name only, by his son Richard; unlike his resolute and determined father, he was a weak and vaccilating ruler, and the Parliament, practically, put him aside; but the manner in which they conducted State affairs became one of so mean and tyrannical a character, that the bulk of the people could no longer submit to it.   The Royalists, too, in the country, were now increasing both in numbers and influence, in addition to which, the Presbyterians also looked with disfavour on the arbitrary proceedings which now characterised the conduct of the Parliament.   This feeling, on the part of both the Royalists and the Presbyterians, at length culminated in a determination to resist by force of arms the ruling power.   Accordingly, an organisation was effected for a simultaneous rising, in different parts of the country, on a given day. The plan, however, was frustrated, with one exception, by Sir Richard Willis, who was in the confidence of the Royalists, having treacherously apprised the party in power of what was intended; and the only enterprise actually attempted was that of seizing the City of Chester, undertaken by Sir George Booth. The Earl of Derby got together a party of Royalists in Lancashire, and headed them in assisting Sir George, but the insurrectionists were defeated by the Parliamentary forces, under the command of Lambert, and a considerable number taken prisoners, amongst them being the Earl of Derby, who remained incarcerated until the Restoration, when he was released from imprisonment along with several others. In the following year, 1661, an event took place in the Isle of Man, which resulted in the Earl of Derby and his illustrious mother, being to a certain extent revenged for the cruel treatment which the dowager Countess had received at the hands of William Christian. In September of that year, Christian was arrested, at the instance of the Earl, on the charge of having treacherously given up the Isle of Man to the Parliament. He was brought to trial on that accusation, and being found guilty, was condemned to death, the sentence being carried out on the 2nd of January, 1662, when the traitor was shot at Hange Hall. Although, as we have already stated, Charles the

Second ungratefully refused the bill passed by Parliament, for restoring the family estates, the Earl ultimately recovered them, and died at Knowsley, on the 21st of December, 1672.

Charles, the eighth Earl of Derby, was succeeded in his title and estates by his son, William, as ninth Earl. Unlike his ancestors, the Earl appears to have taken little or no interest in public matters, but devoted his time, to a great extent, in field sports and other pastimes. He resided alternately at Lathom, Knowsley, and in the Isle of Man, where he largely patronized horse racing. He married Elizabeth, daughter to Thomas, Earl of Ossory, and grand-daughter to the old Duke of Ormonde, and by her he had issue one son, James, Lord Strange, who died at Venice, on his travels, in the 20th year of his age. He had also two daughters, Henrietta and Elizabeth. Henrietta was first married to the Earl of Anglesea, and secondly to John, Lord Ashburnham. Elizabeth died when fourteen years of age. His intention was to re-build and adorn Lathom House, and he had already erected a new front, but he did not live to finish it, and died in 1702, at Chester, when mayor of that city.

The ninth Earl, William, dying without male issue, was succeeded by his brother James, who was in the army, and had for many years been abroad. He was closely attached to William, Prince of Orange, under whom he served during the Prince's campaigns in Flanders. During this Earl's lifetime, and that of his brother, the connexion of the family with Preston became close, and in the year 1688, when the Convocation Parliament sat, he was member of Parliament for that borough. In politics he was a Whig, and warmly supported that party. In the year 1710, when the Whigs, under Marlborough's administration, were expelled from power, the Earl was rather ungraciously removed from the office of Lord Lieutenant of Lancashire, the proceeding being sanctioned by Queen Anne. On the accession, however, of the House of Hanover, he was reinstated in office. In the year 1708, he repaired the family seat at Knowsley, and whilst doing so, in order to mark his sense of the ingratitude of Charles the Second, he caused the following inscription to be carved on a stone in front of it, which remains to the present day: "James, Earl of "Derby, Lord of Man and the Isles, grandson of "James, Earl of Derby, (by Charlotte, daughter of "Claude, Duke of Tremouille,) who was beheaded at "Bolton, 15th of October, 1651, for strenuously ad- "hering to King Charles the Second, who refused a "bill unanimously passed by both Houses of Parlia-

"ment, for restoring to the family the estate he had "lost by his loyalty to him." He married Mary, daughter of Sir William Morley, but had only one son, who died an infant, and the Earl dying without issue, on the 1st February, 1736, the Barony of Strange and the lordship of Man then descended to the Duke of Athol, who, as we have already stated, married a daughter of James, the seventh Earl of Derby; and the earldom itself to the next male heir, Sir Edward Stanley, Bart., of Bickerstaffe, who was descended from Thomas, first Earl of Derby.

The Isle of Man finally reverted to the crown in the reign of George the Third. In 1795 an Act of Parliament was passed, by which the lordship of Man, with all its rights, was purchased by Government from the Duke of Athol and his family, for the sum of £70,000.

———————

Edward, the eleventh Earl, who, as we have just stated, succeeded to the earldom when Sir Edward Stanley, was the son of Sir Thomas Stanley, Bart., M.P. for Preston, in the Parliament of 1695, who married the daughter and heiress of Thomas Patten, Esq., M.P.. for Preston in the Parliament of 1688, and by that marriage, succeeded to considerable property in the neighbourhood of Preston, including the family mansion, "Patten House," in Church Street, in that town, which was for many years afterwards the frequent residence of the Stanley family, and during the guilds, races, and other occasions, the scene of much gaiety and hospitality. Edward the eleventh Earl, was born at his father's residence at Preston, in 1689, where, at that time, the family spent a great portion of their time. Edward (the future Earl) was for some time an alderman of that borough, and served the office of mayor of Preston, in the year 1731-2, when in his forty-second year, and only five years before he became Earl of Derby. The massive silver punch bowl, still used by the corporation on festive occasions, was given by the Earl in 1742, after his resignation of the office of alderman. In 1714 he married Elizabeth, daughter and heiress of Robert Hesketh, of Rufford Hall, near Ormskirk, the ancestor of Sir Thomas George Hesketh, of Rufford Hall, at present M.P. for Preston, in conjunction with the Hon. Frederick Arthur Stanley, second son of the present Earl of Derby. By this marriage he had issue, James, Lord Stanley, born in 1717. Sir Edward was for several years M.P. for the county of Lancaster, and when elevated to the peerage, he was also appointed Lord Lieutenant of the county, which he held for several years, when he resigned the office in favour of his son, Lord Stanley, or Lord Strange, as he was usually called, notwithstanding that that title had descended to the house of Athol. Lord Stanley married the daughter and co-heiress of Hugh Smith, Esq., of Weald Hall, Essex, a very ancient family, on which occasion he assumed the name of Smith Stanley, (which will account for one of the christian names of the present Earl of Derby.)   By this marriage he had issue Edward Smith Stanley, (afterwards twelfth Earl) besides three daughters, Elizabeth, Lucy, and Harriet, who were married respectively to the Rev. Sir Thomas Horton; the Rev. Geoffrey Hornby, rector of Winwick; and Sir Watts Horton, of Chadderton, elder brother of Sir Thomas; two sisters, therefore, being married to two brothers.   In the year 1771, during the life time of his father the Earl, Lord Stanley died, when the former again became Lord Lieutenant of the county, an office which he retained up to the time of his death. His advanced years caused him to live in almost exclusive retirement at Knowsley, where he died on the 23rd of February, 1776, at the ripe old age of 87. It is not a little remarkable that his Countess, who had also arrived at a great age, died almost immediately after her lord, and within two days, they both reposed, side by side, in the family vault at Ormskirk.

CHAPTER VI.

EDWARD, TWELFTH EARL OF DERBY.

EDWARD SMITH STANLEY, son of Lord Stanley who, as we have already stated, died in the lifetime of his father, succeeded his grandfather, as twelfth Earl of Derby, at the early age of 24. The twelfth Earl, was born at the family mansion, "Patten House," in Preston, on the 12th of September, 1752, and, as at the period of his birth, and for some time afterwards, Lord Stanley, otherwise Lord Strange, resided a great deal at Preston, his son, the future Earl, was for many years, a pupil at the grammar school in that town. He subsequently graduated at Trinity College, Cambridge, and at the early age of 22, namely, in the year 1774, he married Lady Elizabeth Hamilton, eldest daughter of James, sixth Duke of Hamilton, at the time still younger than himself, being only in the 21st year of her age. He had issue by her, Edward, (the late Earl) besides two daughters, Charlotte, and Elizabeth Henrietta, the former of whom was married to Edmund Hornby, Esq., son of the Rev. Geoffrey

Hornby, dying on the 25th of November, 1806. The last named daughter was married to S. T. Cole, Esq. It would appear that the Earl's marriage was not in its results a happy one, as he and his Countess afterwards separated.

Although in early life he filled high offices, he did not take any very active part in the affairs of state, but in his political conduct he was ever firm to the Whig instincts and traditions of his family. Immediately after coming of age, he was elected one of the members for the county of Lancaster, which he represented until his elevation to the earldom, when at the same time he was appointed Lord Lieutenant, an office which he held up to the time of his death, extending over a period of more than half a century. He was also appointed one of the ministers during the existence of the government of the Duke of Portland, filling the office of Chancellor of the Duchy of Lancaster in that administration, but he only held the office under that government for a short period. In about twenty-three years afterwards, however—for it was in 1783 that he first held office—he was again made Chancellor of the Duchy, on the formation of the government in which Lord Grey and Lord Holland were prominent members, having consistently given his adherence and support to those distinguished statesmen. Individual distinction and prominence, however, in public and political life, he

did not seem to court for himself, however much he
might afterwards have promoted and encouraged it,
in the persons of his son and his grandsons. He
appeared rather to delight in the splendid hospitalities of the social and private circle, and field sports
had for him greater attractions than any of those
honours which the performance of grave senatorial
duties confer. In his day horse-racing and cock-
fighting were popular and fashionable, confined to
no one class of the community, but shared in and
enjoyed by all; and the act for the prevention of
cruelty to animals not then being in existence, nor
even contemplated by the legislature—indeed had it,
at that period, been brought into the House, the latter
would have unanimously carried a resolution "that the
"bill be read that day six months"—there was no obstacle to the enjoyment, as well in democratic as in
aristocratic circles, of that which was regarded as a
good old English pastime. Accordingly, we find that
the Earl of Derby had one of the best studs, and the
best breed of cocks of any nobleman in the country.
In the enjoyment of the latter sport he was passionately
enthusiastic, personally attending the several "mains"
and race-meetings, more especially at Preston, where he
erected a cock-pit at his own expense—which now, by
the way, has been converted into a temperance hall—
and maintained a noble and liberal hospitality at his
residence, "Patten House," in that town, where he

was always surrounded, during the race week, by a
brilliant circle of the aristocracy of the county. He
also attended the races and "mains" at Liverpool
and other places, in a similar manner, General Yates,
whose breed of cocks was considered equal to that of
his lordship, being almost uniformly his opponent.
Large sums were always staked upon the issue of each
main, by his Lordship and the General, a thousand
guineas being the ordinary amount, but there were
several occasions on which the mains were fought for
as much as two and even three thousand guineas.

On the 14th of March, 1797, his wife, from whom
he had been separated for several years, died, and in
a short time afterwards, on the 1st of May, in the
same year, he was married to the celebrated Miss
Farren, who became his second Countess. It is due
to his Lordship's memory, as well as to that of Miss
Farren, to state that his attachment to that gifted
lady was of a purely honourable and affectionate
character, which was testified by the fact that even
before the marriage, but more especially after it, she
was received in the highest circles, and was recognised and cordially welcomed at court. She had the
reputation of being not less amiable than talented,
and her society was sought and enjoyed by all who
could appreciate intellectual acquirements, or admire
the most exalted virtues. By his second Countess the
Earl had issue, a daughter, still-born, on the 27th of

March, 1798; Lucy Elizabeth, born 12th March, 1799, died 27th April, 1809, in the eleventh year of her age, and buried at Ormskirk; James Smith Stanley, born 9th March, 1800, died 3rd April, 1817, aged 17, and buried at Ormskirk; and Mary Margaret, born 23rd March, 1801, married 29th November, 1821, to Thomas Egerton, second and present Earl of Wilton. She died in 1860. The Countess of Derby died on the 23rd of April, 1829, and the Earl's death took place on the 21st of October, 1834, in the 83rd year of his age, and they were both interred in the family vault at Ormskirk.

The Earl's funeral, which took place on the 31st of October, ten days after his death, was conducted with much pomp and ceremony, and was very numerously attended by all classes of the community connected with the county. It was the wish of the family, who were desirous of carrying out the directions of the deceased Earl, that his interment should take place with all the privacy that his rank might admit of, but the lengthened period during which he had enjoyed the earldom, extending over nearly sixty years, and the universal popularity and respect in which he had been held during a life unusually prolonged, caused the funeral to be attended by a considerable number of the aristocracy and other residents within the county palatine, who were anxious to accompany the noble Earl's remains to their last

earthly resting place; and the carriages and other
vehicles which joined the mournful cortege as it
emerged from the Stanley Gate entrance to Knowsley,
were upwards of sixty in number. The shops and
other places of business in Ormskirk were closed
during the day; the blinds were drawn down in most,
if not all the private houses; and, throughout the
town, every outward manifestation of mourning was
shown. Large numbers of strangers came into the
town from all parts of the county; the inn yards, and
even the several streets, being crowded with carriages
and vehicles of every description. The church was
filled some hours before the funeral procession arrived
at the sacred edifice, every seat being occupied, and
several hundreds were unable to obtain admission.
The funeral cortege left the hall at nine o'clock in the
morning, headed by four mutes on horseback, with
pages on each side. These were followed by the
tenants on the Knowsley estate, two hundred and
eighty in number, riding on black horses, and wearing
hat bands and scarfs. To these succeeded the household servants, walking two abreast. Four mourning
coaches followed, containing respectively the deceased
Earl's physicians, clergymen, and the pall bearers,
with four pages on each side of the coaches. Two
mutes on horseback again succeeded, followed by his
lordship's coronet and cushion, on a state horse. Next
came the body, borne in a hearse drawn by six horses,

with heraldic insignia. Four mourning coaches, each drawn by four horses, followed, the first coach containing the chief mourners, namely, the Earl of Derby, son of the deceased Earl, and his grandsons, Lord Stanley, the Hon. Henry Thomas Stanley, and the Hon. Charles James Fox Stanley. The three other mourning coaches contained the Earl of Wilton, the Hon. Richard Bootle Wilbraham, Edmund George Hornby, Esq., Colonel Hornby, Edmund Hornby, Esq., Edward Penhryn, Esq., Captain Hornby, Adam Hodgson, Esq., the Rev. F. Hopwood, Rev. G. Hornby, Rev. J. J. Hornby, and the Rev. E. James. The four mourning coaches just named were immediately followed by the deceased Earl's carriage, drawn by six horses, the Earl of Derby's carriage, and Lord Stanley's carriage, each drawn by four horses, and all closed. On the cortege arriving at Stanley Gate, about two miles and a half from Ormskirk, it was joined by the general procession, consisting of thirty-six private carriages, containing the members of the leading families of the county, and other gentlemen, amongst them being the Mayor of Liverpool, and the Rev. Jonathan Brookes and the Rev. Augustus Campbell, Rectors of Liverpool. On the procession arriving at the church, about eleven o'clock in the forenoon, the body was met by the Rev. Joshua Thomas Horton, vicar of Ormskirk, who performed the funeral service. The pall bearers were Lord Skelmersdale, the Marquis

of Westminster, Lord Molyneux, Sir Thos. Dalrymple
Hesketh, Bart., Colonel Rawstorne, W. Egerton, Esq.,
W. Hulton, Esq., and R. G. Hopwood, Esq.   The
hearse in which the body was borne was most elaborately finished, and very costly.   The outline was
somewhat tomb-like, with columns at the angles, and
its draperies were most beautifully ornamented and
embellished with superb fringes, tassels, and plumes.
Placed in compartments there were ten escutcheons,
bearing the arms of the deceased, with the quarterings
of the various alliances, and on the horse-palls appeared coronets, showing the deceased's dignity.   The
coffin was covered with rich crimson silk velvet, ornamented with massive silver handles, chased like coronets.   On the lid there was a fine chased ornament,
emblematic of life and eternity, with a large silver plate,
bearing the following inscription :—"The Right Hon.
"Edward Smith Stanley, twelfth Earl of Derby, born
"September 12, 1752, died October 21, 1834."   When
the coffin was deposited in its place in the vault, the
herald went down, and placed the coronet and cushion
on the lid.

   The Earl was succeeded in his title and estates
by his son Edward, who became thirteenth Earl.

CHAPTER VII.

EDWARD, THIRTEENTH EARL OF DERBY.

EDWARD, thirteenth Earl, who was born on the 21st of April, 1775, married, in the year 1798, his cousin, Charlotte Margaret, second daughter of the Rev. Geoffrey Hornby, by whom he had issue, Edward George Geoffrey Smith Stanley, (now fourteenth Earl,) the Hon. Henry Thomas Stanley, and the Hon. Charles James Fox Stanley; besides four daughters, namely, Charlotte Elizabeth, married in 1823, to Edward Penrhyn, Esq., and died in 1853; Emily Lucy, who died in infancy; Louisa Emily, married in 1825, to Lieutenant-Colonel Samuel Long, but died in December following; and Ellinor Mary, married to the Rev. Frank George Hopwood, the present rector of Winwick. In the year 1796, on the dissolution of Parliament, and immediately after attaining his majority, he was elected a member of Parliament for the borough of Preston, under circumstances which it may be interesting here to record. For several years before this election, extending, indeed, to nearly half a century backwards, the Derby family and the Corporation had been constantly at issue, as to whether the former or the latter should nominate the members for Preston, and the contests were always severe, invariably resulting, however, in the election of the Earl's nominees, against those of the Corporation. For a period of nearly thirty years, namely, from 1768 to 1795, the borough was, with one exception, exclusively represented by General Burgoyne, (who, while a subaltern in a marching regiment, stationed in Preston, contracted a secret marriage with Lady Charlotte Stanley, a daughter of the eleventh Earl of Derby,) and Sir Henry Hoghton, Bart., the candidates in the interest of the Derby family. The exception to which we have alluded was, that on the death of General Burgoyne, in 1792, he was succeeded in the representation by Mr. William Cunliffe Shawe, who, like his predecessors, came into Parliament under the Whig or Derby interest. We have already stated that at the general election, in 1796, the subject of our present notice, then Lord Stanley, became a candidate, in conjunction with Sir Henry Philip Hoghton, Mr. Shawe having retired. The Corporation, on this occasion, made a determined stand against the Derby interest, bringing forward as their candidate in the Tory, and, as they expressed it, the "manufacturing interest," Mr. John Horrocks, the head of the now wide-world-known and celebrated manufacturing firm of Horrocks, Miller, & Co. Mr. Horrocks at that time employed a considerable number of work-people in the town, and was a person of much wealth and local influence. The contest was an exceedingly severe one, and personal and party feeling ran very high. The poll was kept open for eleven days, during the first eight of which Mr. Horrocks was each day at the head. On the ninth day, however, he fell to the second; on the tenth he was at the bottom of the poll; and on the morning of the eleventh, he retired, when the numbers were—Stanley, 772; Houghton, 756; Horrocks, 742. At this election the celebrated Lord Abinger, chief Baron of the Exchequer, but at that time plain Mr. Scarlett, acted as "assistant" to the Mayor, and was paid 200 guineas for his services. A memorandum appears in the books of the Corporation, to the effect that that body borrowed the money from Mr. Pedder, a banker, and gave a bond for the amount. In order to show the intensity of the hostile feeling which at this time existed between the Derby family and the Corporation, in reference to the representation of the borough, we quote the following extract from an able and interesting little work, on the "History of the Parliamentary Representation of Preston, during the last hundred years," by William Dobson :—"While," says the author "the Derbyite nominees were the

"members, they were never, except one of them on a
"single occasion, solicited to take charge of any
"of the numerous addresses, which the Corporation
"were accustomed to present to the throne. Mr. Black-
"burne, the Tory member for the county, was always
"selected to be the medium of the corporate solicita-
"tions reaching the ears of royalty.   Not merely was
"the feeling of hostility between the rival competitors
"for political influence carried into the business of
"the town, but even into its pleasures, and for six
"years, from 1786 to 1791, races were held under the
"auspices of each party, the Corporation races being
"held on Preston Moor; the Earl of Derby's races, as
"an opposition meeting, on Fulwood Moor, a lease of
"which had been obtained from the Duchy of Lancas-
"ter.   The political differences which divided the
"town extended even to sedan chairs.   The coats of
"the chairmen had collars of the colour of one or
"other of the two great parties, and as the ladies
"were equally warm in their political sympathies as
"the rougher sex, they showed their predilection, not
"only in the ribbons they wore, but in the choice of
"their sedans.   A lady of the family of Pedder, or
"Starkie, or Gorst, would have walked home in a
"thunder storm before she would have been carried
"in a Derby or Burgoyne chair, while the wives and
"damsels of the Shaws, the Hornbys, and · the
"Whiteheads, would have missed going to the best

"ball of the season, rather than have been taken there
"in a Corporation sedan."

In the next election, which took place in 1802,
Lord Stanley was again elected member for Preston,
but under circumstances altogether dissimilar to those
which we have just recorded. There were two reasons
why it was deemed advisable that a different state of
things to that which had so long existed should
prevail. On the one hand the election struggles
between the Corporation and the Derby interests respectively, had involved the former in certain expenses
which, if not actually illegal, were at least not credit-
able to a public body; while, on the other hand, the
influence of Mr. Horrocks had so largely increased, in
consequence of his energy and enterprise in extending
the cotton trade in the town, that a compromise
between the two parties was recommended, and
ultimately carried into effect; the terms of arrangement being that the Derby family should nominate
one member, and the Corporation and manufacturing
interest the other, and that each should support
the other in carrying out the bargain. This questionable arrangement, which we must say, displays
an absence of political dignity on both sides, inasmuch
as parties diametrically opposed to each other were
now to work together against any independent candidate whose views might be in accord with either of the
coalition candidates, was nevertheless gravely reduced

to writing, and signed by the "high contracting parties,"
for it is recorded in Baines's History of Lancashire,
that " this coalition was made through the intervention
" of Thomas Butterworth Bagley, Esq., of Hope, near
" Manchester, and ratified by the signatures of eleven
" gentlemen in Preston, the leaders of the parties, to
" a written agreement prepared for the purpose."
Under it, Lord Stanley, the Whig, and Mr. John
Horrocks, the Tory, were returned unopposed at the
election in 1802, Sir Henry Hoghton having retired.
Mr. John Horrocks, however, died in 1804, when he
was succeeded by his brother Mr. Samuel Horrocks.
The next election was in 1806, when Lord Stanley
and Mr. Samuel Horrocks were again elected under
the " compact ;" and in the following year, 1807, when
the Parliament was dissolved, they a third time
presented themselves, and were, as before, returned
unopposed. The absence of high political principle
involved in this arrangement, was frequently severely
commented upon by the journalists of the time, and
one writer, referring to the position of Lord Stanley
and Mr. Horrocks under the terms to which they
respectively became parties, somewhat satirically
remarks, "Although they scarcely ever voted on the
" same side in the House of Commons, they had in
" Preston one committee, they canvassed together, and
" strange as it would now seem, subscribed their
" names to the same address." This remarkable

"coalition," however, although several times assailed
by independent candidates and their friends, who did
not approve of such a Whig and Tory combination,
was successful at every general election which took
place after the agreement, and it was only in the year
1826, when the present Earl of Derby, then Mr.
Stanley, first became a candidate for Preston, that it
was broken through.   In 1812 Lord Stanley resigned
his seat for Preston, in order to become a candidate
for Lancashire, in place of his relative Colonel Stanley,
who then retired from Parliament.   He continued
to represent the county until 1832, when he was called
to the House of Peers, in his father's life time, by the
title of Baron Stanley, of Bickerstaffe.   He never made
any prominent display whilst in Parliament, but during
the whole of that period, both in the House of
Commons and in the Peers, he was a firm and
consistent supporter of the Whigs.   For several years
before his death he ceased to take much interest
in public affairs, and occupied the most of his time in
increasing and enriching his menagerie and aviary at
Knowsley.   He was devotedly attached to zoology, a
science which he largely pursued.   He was for several
years president of the Linnæan and Zoological Societies,
and his collection of mammalia, birds, and objects of
natural history and zoology at Knowsley was the largest,
most varied, and most valuable in the kingdom, consisting of specimens from all parts of the world.   The main-

tenance of his menagerie and aviary, which necessitated
the occupation of one hundred acres of land within
Knowsley Park, in addition to a water space of seventy
acres, is said to have cost him upwards of £15,000 a
year, and the probability of the truth of this may be
imagined when we state that he had agents in almost
every known country, who were constantly purchasing
for him living, as well as dead specimens of all kinds
and species, which they forwarded to him at Knowsley,
to be added to his already extensive collection there.
The number of mammalia in the collection consisted
of 94 species, containing 345 individuals, of which no
less than 39 species and 207 individuals were bred at
Knowsley.   The collection of birds was numerous and
varied, consisting, exclusive of poultry, of 318 species
and 1272 individuals, and of this number 45 species
and 549 individuals were bred at Knowsley.   Thus the
total number of mammalia and birds in the collection amounted to 412 species and 1617 individuals.
The extensive area appropriated for the accom-
modation of the several specimens was exceedingly well arranged, the mammalia having ample
space and shelter in large paddocks, whilst the
birds had also a spacious run under wired covers.   The
animals comprised rare and costly specimens from
almost every foreign country ; amongst them being
the female yak, (*Poëphagus grunniens*,) a native of
Thibet, as also a hybrid bull of the same species, like-

wise from Thibet.   There is a peculiarity about the
yak which can scarcely be said to apply to any other
animal.   It was affirmed, at the time when the Earl's
aviary was in existence, that it was the only species of
domesticated-cattle that had not then extended beyond
its natural boundary. The specimen in the Knowsley
collection resembled in size a small English ox,
its very long hair and large bushy tail giving it
a somewhat remarkable appearance.   When the
Nepaulese Ambassador visited this country, he brought
with him several presents for the Queen; amongst
them being the *chowry*, or cow-tail fan, which in
Nepaul is an appendage of royalty.   These fans were
from the tail of the yak, which is composed of a tuft
of long silky hair.   There were also several specimens
of the Brahmin zebu and Arab bull and cow, (*Bos
Taurus*.)   The Brahmin cattle were largely turned to
practical account by the late Earl, the valuable cross
between them and the English short-horns being first
introduced by his lordship, and it may be added that
the breed is still maintained on the Knowsley estate.
The collection also included both male and female
Bara Singha deer, (*Cervus Axis?*) *Duvaucellii, Cervus
Elaphoides*, or *Cervus Duvaucellii*,) being the only
living specimens in the country at the time, with
the exception of one in the Zoological Gardens,
London.   There was also a fine elk, (*Cervus Alces
palmatus*,) from North America.   It was a specimen

of the largest of the deer species, which is much
prized by the American hunter for its flesh.
Amongst the antelopes were the male and female
gnu (*Antilope Gnu*), from South Africa; also two
male and three female elands, (*Antilope Orcas*),
which were then the only living specimens in this
country, one of them being bred at Knowsley. The
eland is the largest of the antelope species; when
full grown it measures five feet in height at the
shoulder, and in consequence of its docile character,
and the rich quality of its flesh, it is more prized
than any of the wild animals of South Africa. There
were also in the collection eight Indian antelopes,
(*Capra cervicapra*,) one male and seven females, being
the only herd ever brought to this country; besides
several llamas, zebras, kangaroos, rodents, lemurs,
armadillos, and a great variety of foreign goats,
sheep, and dogs.

The aviary included a splendid collection of
vultures, eagles, emus, ostriches, parrots and parroquets,
including the masked parrots from the South Sea
Islands, being the only living birds of the kind in the
country; bustards, East India cassowary, cranes,
and pelicans. There were also in the collection six
black-necked swans from South America, of a rare
and valuable species, being the only living specimens
ever brought to this country, also five Impeyan
pheasants, male and female, from the Himalaya

Mountains, a most gorgeous species ; game of all kinds, including partridge and grouse, and in addition, a numerous collection of poultry.

The Earl had also a splendid museum, containing several thousand specimens, and consisting of animals and birds which had died in the menagerie and aviary at Knowsley, besides several other specimens obtained by collectors, at the cost of his lordship, in almost every part of the world. One of the most valuable birds in the museum was the apteryx, or wingless bird of New Zealand, being the first specimen ever brought to Europe. This interesting and remarkable bird was brought to England in 1812, from the South Coast of New Zealand, by Captain Barclay, of the ship Providence. On his arrival in this country, Captain Barclay presented it to Dr. Shaw, one of the most prominent and able naturalists of the day. After it came into Dr. Shaw's possession, he described it at great length in the 24th volume of his own magazine, the *Naturalist's Miscellany.* At the doctor's death, the late Earl of Derby purchased the bird, and, as doubts had been thrown on the existence of such a specimen, the Earl forwarded it to the exhibition of the Linnæan Society. The materials with which it was stuffed were previously removed by the Earl's directions, and afterwards the skin was closely and minutely examined, which had the effect of finally dissipating the doubts

of those who had been sceptical as to its existence.
The museum, which was one of the most extensive
and varied in the country, consisted of 611 stuffed
quadrupeds, and 11,131 stuffed birds, in addition to
which there were 607 quadrupeds, and 7700 birds
unstuffed, making a total of 1218 quadrupeds, and
18,831 birds, or a grand total of 20,049; and besides
the above named, there was also a large collection of
eggs, and a considerable number of reptiles and fishes.
Liverpool has great reason to be proud of his lordship, and honour and revere his memory, for at his
death, which took place at Knowsley, on the 2nd of
July, 1851, in the 77th year of his age, he bequeathed
the whole of this splendid and unrivalled museum
to the mayor and corporation of that town, in trust
for the benefit of the inhabitants, and the magnificent
collection is deposited in that part of the Free Library
now known as the Derby Museum.

Although the last years of the Earl's life were
passed in retirement at Knowsley, and to a great
extent occupied in his favourite study of zoology, he
at the same time devoted much of his time and attention to projects for the employment of labour for the
improvement of his estates and the benefit of his
tenantry. He ever showed much consideration and
sympathy for his servants and labourers, as the following interesting and touching circumstance will show.
It was his lordship's custom to pay a visit of inspec-

tion over different portions of the Knowsley estates
almost daily, and one day, whilst so engaged, he met a
foreman in a distant part of the park, and finding the
workmen absent he enquired of the foreman where
they were, when the foreman replied, "rather too
frosty, my lord, to do a fair day's work;" on which
his lordship immediately rejoined, "poor men must
live, frost or no frost, as well as other men!" and he
ordered the foreman to re-call the whole of the men
and set them to some kind of employment or other.

His lordship was interred in the family vault, at
Ormskirk, on Tuesday, the 8th of July, the funeral
procession being very imposing and more than a mile
in length. After the Earl's death, the body was placed
in an apartment known as "the Earl's room," where it
reposed until it was removed to its final resting place.
The arrangements of the room imparted to it a
strikingly solemn appearance. The floor was covered
with black cloth, and a black railing encircled the
coffin, which was surrounded by plumes of ostrich
feathers, these being again surrounded by immense
wax candles, in silver candelabra. The coffin was
made from an oak tree, that grew in Knowsley Park,
and which had been a favourite with the deceased
Earl.

The general procession was formed at Stanley
Gate, about two miles and a half from Ormskirk. It
was headed by several mutes on horseback, accom-

panied by pages. After these came his lordship's tenants, to the number of three hundred, all mounted on black horses, and wearing hat bands and scarfs. Then followed the several heads of departments at the hall, and other servants, both in and out of livery. Three mourning coaches, each drawn by four horses, succeeded, containing, respectively, the clergy, the medical attendants of the deceased, and the Earl's several agents connected with the management of the Knowsley and other estates.. Following these, again, were the coronet and cushion, on a state horse, richly and fully caparisoned. Then came the body, in a hearse drawn by six horses, attended by bearers with six truncheons on each side. It was immediately followed by a mourning coach, drawn by four horses, containing the chief mourners, namely, the present Earl of Derby; his brother, the Hon. Charles James Fox Stanley; and his son, Lord Stanley. Five other mourning coaches followed, all drawn by four horses, and containing, respectively, the immediate relatives and friends of the family, including Admiral Hornby, Colonel Hornby, Captain Wyndham Hornby, Captain Geoffery Hornby, Edward George Hornby, Esq., the Rev. Edward Hornby, Rev. William Hornby, Rev. W. Hopwood, Rev. Phipps Champneys, Colonel Long, the Earl of Wilton, the Earl of Sefton, the Hon. Colonel Wilbraham, L. Penhryn, Esq., O. Penhryn, Esq., Adam Hodgson, Esq., the Rev. Ellis Ashton, and the Rev.

Thomas Ashton. The deceased Earl's carriage, drawn
by six horses, and the present Earl's carriage, drawn
by four horses, and both closed, completed the procession direct from the hall, but a considerable number
of private carriages followed. The pall bearers were
the Earl of Sefton, the Hon. Colonel Wilbraham, the
Rev. William Hornby, Adam Hodgson, Esq., the Rev.
Ellis Ashton, and the Rev. Thomas Ashton. The
funeral service was read by the Rev. R. Rawstorne, vicar
of Ormskirk, after which the body was deposited in
the family vault inside the church, and laid by the
side of the Earl's Countess. It is probable that the
deceased Earl will be the last of the family buried at
Ormskirk, the vault being now full. A new one
has been constructed at Knowsley Church, which,
it is understood, will be the future place of sepulture
of the Stanley family.

In a few months after the Earl's death, his rich
and extensive aviary and menagerie was disposed of
by public auction, and its world-wide celebrity brought
to Knowsley large numbers of connoisseurs and purchasers, not only from all parts of England, but from
France and other Continental nations. The sale took
place in accordance with the will of the deceased Earl,
who ordered that the collection should be sold, after
her Majesty and the Zoological Society of London had
exercised the privilege he had extended to them, of
selecting each any animal or bird from the entire

collection. The Queen selected two of the black-
necked swans, and the five Impeyan pheasants; and
the Zoological Society chose the lot of Eland antelopes. It may here be stated that the elands continued to breed so freely in the Zoological Gardens in
London, that it became necessary to dispose of their
surplus stock, which was principally sold to Viscount
Hill, of Hawkstone, Shropshire, who has since bred
them with equal success, and a fine fatted specimen
was exhibited at the Christmas cattle show, 1867, in
the Agricultural Hall, Islington, where it was purchased by an enterprising butcher, but who found
it after all more profitable to sell it as a zoological
specimen than as the dishes of beef or venison.
The sale commenced on Monday, the 6th of October,
and extended over that week and the following
Monday, occupying altogether seven days. Although,
as we have already stated, purchasers attended
from several foreign countries, the proceeds of the
sale were little more than nominal as compared
with the cost of this magnificent collection, the
aggregate amount of which can never be ascertained.
The sum received was only about £7000, being not
even equal to the annual expense of the maintenance and keep of the collection. The prices realised
were thus much below the value of the several
specimens, but some of them were sold for a considerable amount, including the male and female

gnu, which fetched £233 10s.; the male and female leucoryx, £122; and two zebras, £140 and £150 each. The eight Indian antelopes were sold to Lord Hill, for £85, and his lordship was also a large purchaser of other specimens. Several of the lots were purchased for the Queen, and amongst the other principal purchasers were the Zoological Society of London, the Earl of Ellesmere, Count Demidoff, and M. Vichman, of Antwerp.

His lordship was succeeded by Edward George Geoffrey Smith Stanley, the present distinguished Earl, whose brilliant political and public career we shall now proceed to narrate.

CHAPTER VIII.

THE RIGHT HON. EDWARD, FOURTEENTH EARL OF DERBY, K.G., PRIME MINISTER.

EDWARD, thirteenth Earl of Derby, was succeeded in his title and estates, by Edward George Geoffery Smith Stanley, the fourteenth, and present Earl, who now occupies, for the third time, the dignified and high position of her Majesty's Prime Minister. It may truly be said that the public career of the present Earl, who next to James, the "Great Stanley," is the most illustrious and distinguished of this illustrious house, embraces the political history of this country for nearly half a century past, and is identified with some of the most remarkable and memorable events in her political past.

The talented subject of our present notice, now at the head of the government of the country, was born on the 29th of March, 1799, at the family seat at Knowsley. The Honourable Edward Geoffery Smith Stanley, (for by this name and title we must for

the present designate him,) was, when yet young, sent
to Eton, where he received the earlier portion of his
education.   He was thence removed to Christ Church,
Oxford, where he soon distinguished himself, in ver-
sification and classical attainments, obtaining, in
1819, the chancellor's prize for Latin verse, the
composition which gained him this honour, and which
he read according to custom in the Sheldonian theatre,
being entitled "Syracuse." He thus won great distinction at the early age of twenty.

In the year 1822, two years after he attained his
majority, he was elected member for Stockbridge,
entering Parliament as an adherent of those high
Whig principles which his family had so long held
and maintained. For two years after he was elected a
member of the House he had the prudence, as a young
member, to maintain a judicious silence, but this was
not because he had not the ability to address the
Parliament with eloquence and effect, for it is recorded
of him that at the early age of nineteen he revealed the
possession of those brilliant rhetorical powers for which
he has now been so long pre-eminently distinguished,
having on the occasion of a banquet at Preston, spoken
in a manner which commanded the admiration of all
who heard him. His maiden speech, in Parliament,
however, was not delivered until 1824, when upon
the 30th of March in that year, he addressed the
House on the Manchester Gas Light bill, which, on

that night, was brought forward. His speech, which was directed against the measure, elicited the marked approbation of the House, more especially of that great authority, Sir James Mackintosh, who, immediately on Mr. Stanley resuming his seat rose, and said :—

"I have heard, with the greatest pleasure, the "speech which has just been delivered by my honour- "able young friend behind me—a speech which must "have given the highest satisfaction to all who heard "it, and which affords the strongest promise that the "talents which the honourable member has displayed "in supporting the local interests of his constituents, "will be exerted with equal ardour and effect in "maintaining the rights and interests of the country. "No man could have witnessed with greater satisfac- "tion than myself an accession to the talents of this "house which is calculated to give lustre to its "character, and strengthen its influence; and it is "more particularly a subject of satisfaction to me, "when I reflect that those talents are likely to be "employed in supporting principles which I conscien- "tiously believe to be most beneficial to the country."

In the same session of Parliament, and not long after the maiden speech to which we have just referred, Mr. Stanley again prominently displayed not only his great oratorical powers, but likewise those administrative abilities by which he has since been distinguished. This was on the question of the Irish Church establishment, in reference to which, when in office, he took such a leading position.

On the 31st of May, 1825, he married the Hon. Emma Caroline, second daughter of Edward Bootle Wilbraham, first Baron Skelmersdale, by whom he had issue Edward Henry, Lord Stanley, at present member for King's Lynn, and also Chief Secretary for Foreign Affairs in his father's administration; Lady Emma Charlotte married to the Hon. Colonel Talbot, brother of the Earl of Shrewsbury; and the Hon. Frederick Arthur Stanley, M.P. for Preston, for which town he was elected at the last general election in 1865; and who recently married Lady Constance Villiers, second daughter of the Earl of Clarendon. In addition to the above named the Earl and Countess had two sons and a daughter, who died in infancy.

In the year 1826, a general election took place, when Mr. Hornby, Mr. Stanley's relative, as well as Mr. Horrocks, his colleague, both resigned their seats for Preston; and as the Corporation at that time wisely resolved to interfere no more in their official capacity, with the elections, the notorious "coalition" to which we have already alluded, and which for twenty-four years had kept the representation of the borough exclusively in its hands, was at an end. The constituency, moreover, was now so large as not to be easily influenced and controlled, although, from

the effect of old associations, there were yet large
numbers of the inhabitants willing to vote, and shout,
and throw up their hats for "my Lord and the
"Corporation." On the occasion of this election,
Mr. Stanley resigned his seat at Stockbridge, and
became a candidate for Preston, professing those
same Whig principles with which his family had
ever been identified in the representation of the
borough. In his address to the electors he declared
that he was not connected with any other candidate,
and added that he was "unassisted by any other
"influence, and unfettered by any other connexion."
This election excited an unusual amount of interest
throughout the country, and amongst other causes
which led to this, was the notoriety of one of the
candidates. The Radicals introduced the noted
politician and author, William Cobbett, who had
frequently been imprisoned for the public expression
of seditious language, and whom it was popularly
thought that the "people" desired to see in Parliament. The second candidate who appeared in
the field was the late Mr. John Wood, a barrister,
(son of Mr. Ottiwell Wood, then well known as
a Liverpool celebrity) who was afterwards Chairman of the Board of Inland Revenue, and who
was supposed to seek the suffrages of the electors
on Liberal principles a little more advanced then
those professed by Mr. Stanley. The other candidate,

making four in all, was Captain Barrie, R.N., who came forward in the interest of the Conservatives. The several candidates were thus totally distinct from, and independent of, each other, although it was understood that Mr. Wood would, to a great extent, have the support of Mr. Stanley's friends. Universal suffrage, also then prevailed in Preston, every resident male adult having a vote. At that time, moreover, the polling extended to fifteen days, and so determined was the contest that the poll was kept open to the last moment. Day by day, as Mr. Stanley continued to head the poll, with Mr. Wood, second on the list, the state of public feeling increased in intensity. Speeches were made at the close of each day's voting by the several candidates, in the course of which Mr. Stanley and Mr. Cobbett had many salient encounters with each other, the latter attacking the former, on the ground of his aristocratic connexions, in terms far more expressive than polite. Mr. Cobbett's language, indeed, towards Mr. Stanley, throughout the entire struggle, was coarse and vituperative, abounding in the most insulting epithets and allusions towards the Knowsley family, but the demagogue and then idol of the *vox populi*, was altogether unequal to the cutting and disdainful satire of the young Whig patrician, whose scathing denunciations of his jacobite antagonist, even at that early age, revealed his brilliant talents. The political tergiver-

sations and inconsistencies of the great Radical
agitator were laid bare before the electors daily
during the contest, in a publication called the "Political Mountebank," and the manner in which
Mr. Stanley analyzed and dissected these issues, to
the prejudice of Mr. Cobbett, caused the latter to
wince under the castigation, whilst it inspired feelings
of enthusiastic admiration on the part of Mr. Stanley's
numerous friends and supporters.   On the third day
of the election the town was in such a state of
excitement that the authorities became alarmed.
The windows of the Bull Hotel, Mr. Stanley's head-
quarters, were destroyed by the mob, and in retaliation
a similar attack was made upon the Castle and
Waterloo Hotels, where Mr. Cobbett and Captain
Barrie were respectively staying.   The riot increasing,
and there being every prospect of the town being
placed at the mercy of the populace, a detachment
of the 1st Dragoon Guards, which was billeted at
Kirkham, a few miles distant, was sent for, and in a
short time the cavalry galloped into the town and
dispersed the mob, who were then engaged in their
work of destruction, several persons being apprehended
and taken prisoners.

The people, who knew that the military were at
Kirkham, were astounded at the quick advent of the
soldiers, but a scheme, and a very ingenious one,
was devised, whereby to make known to them at

Kirkham that their presence was required to suppress any riot. The signal was a flag, to be hoisted on the staff upon the church steeple, which could be distinctly seen at Kirkham, and an observer was placed there to watch, and at every five minutes to report whether any signal was made. The signal was given in Preston at ten minutes after five in the afternoon, and seen in Kirkham in five minutes afterwards, and the dragoons immediately mounted and galloped to Preston, where they arrived in forty minutes after starting, the distance being nine miles. On the following morning a body of foot guards came into the town, and the presence of the military was denounced by Mr. Cobbett and others as a gross violation of the liberty of the subject. The Preston *Chronicle*, of the 17th June, the week after the election, says that "the military were sent for, not "on account of these outrages, which the civil power "could have coped with, but to protect the power- "loom factories, information having been sworn to by "some individuals that an attack was meditated upon "them that evening, a fact which the great influx of "the country people in the course of the day tended "to support. The power-looms were then being generally introduced, and like all improvements in machinery tending to economise labour, they were unpopular with the masses, and there had been in various parts of the country riots and destruction of these machines, where millowners had commenced working with them. At length, on the fifteenth day, being the full time allowed by law, this memorable contest was brought to a close, when Mr. Stanley and Mr. Wood were elected, the former by an overwhelming majority, the numbers being, for Mr. Stanley, 2,944; Wood, 1,974; Barrie, 1,653; Cobbett, 995.

The year after his election for Preston, in April, 1827, Mr. Stanley joined the administration then formed by Mr. Canning. Mr. Robinson, afterwards Lord Goderich, filled the office of Chief Secretary for the Colonies in that government, and Mr. Stanley was appointed Under Secretary. The Premier's lamented death in four months after the formation of his ministry, led to a reconstruction of the cabinet, Lord Goderich being appointed Premier. He was succeeded in his office as Chief Secretary for the Colonies, by the Right Hon. William Huskisson, Mr. Stanley retaining his position as Under Secretary during the brief period of that ministry's existence.

At the commencement of 1828—for the ministry only remained office for a period of about five months —the Duke of Wellington's government was formed, and the Tory party, headed by the "Iron Duke," with Sir Robert Peel as his lieutenant, held the reins of power until the close of 1830.

Mr. Stanley, who, during this last-named period, was in the ranks of the Opposition, distinguished

himself on several occasions by his eloquent advocacy
of the various measures then proposed by Earl Grey,
and the other great Whig leaders, and his speeches
in favour of Catholic emancipation, the repeal of the
Test and Corporation Acts, Parliamentary Reform,
and other great liberal measures, established for him
a reputation as one of the most rising young
statesmen of the day. In July, 1830, the death of
George the Fourth led to a dissolution of Parliament,
when Mr. Stanley again presented himself as a
candidate at Preston, along with his colleague
Mr. Wood. On this occasion there was no opposition
to the re-election of the late members, with the
exception of Mr. Henry Hunt, the blacking manu-
facturer, and great Radical, of Peterloo notoriety. He
retired, however, on the fourth day of polling, the
numbers being, for Mr. Stanley, 2,998; Wood, 2,489;
Hunt, 1,308; Mr. Stanley and Mr. Wood having
thus been re-elected

The result of the general election, on the occasion
of the King's death, strengthened the hands of the
Whig and Reform party, and led to the downfall of
the Wellington-Peel administration, on the 20th of
November; when Earl Grey was sent for by King
William, and his Majesty entrusted to the then leader
of the great Whig party, the formation of a new
ministry. In that administration, Mr. Stanley was
included, his eminent services to the Whigs being

acknowledged by his appointment to the highly responsible office of Chief Secretary for Ireland. Having so accepted office, he vacated his seat for Preston, and again presented himself for re-election. This was the most memorable event appertaining to Mr. Stanley's election experiences, and unexpectedly severed his political connexion with Preston. In a few days after his address had been issued, the friends and supporters of Mr. Hunt, the extreme Radical, again put forward his name; but Mr. Stanley's committee looked upon the opposition without any feelings of apprehension as to the safety of the right honourable gentleman's seat. At the close of the first day's polling, however, Mr. Stanley's committee were astounded to find Mr. Hunt in a considerable majority, the numbers being for Mr. Hunt, 1204; for Mr. Stanley, 791. The second and third day's polling increased, although slightly, Mr. Hunt's majority, and the excitement of the contest had now risen to such a pitch as to have extended far beyond the boundaries of the borough. Day after day the town was crowded with large numbers of operatives and others from the different manufacturing districts of Lancashire, whose sympathies were enlisted on behalf of the extreme Radical candidate. The Huntites had monster processions every day, accompanied by numerous large banners, flags, and bands of music; these processions usually taking place in the evening, between the hours of seven and ten o'clock, when a number of burning tar barrels were introduced into the procession, illuminating the public thoroughfares in the darkness of the night. The authorities appeared powerless to restrain the reckless enthusiasm of the populace, and for the time the latter might almost be said to have had possession of the town. Mr. Hunt's speeches to the mob abounded in the most violent and intemperate language towards Mr. Stanley and the classes he represented, which had the effect of still further increasing the great excitement that prevailed. Mr. Hunt's majority was considerably reduced during the subsequent days of the polling, but still he kept at the head of the poll, and his friends appeared determined, at all hazards, that he should be elected, for at the polling booth they commenced a system of intimidation, and resorted to other obstructive measures which prevented numbers of Mr. Stanley's supporters from recording their votes. Mr. Nicholas Grimshaw, a very warm Tory, was mayor of the borough at the time, and the feeling of partizanship, as against Mr. Stanley, which he displayed during the whole of the contest, excited intense indignation in the town, and caused his worship to become very unpopular with the middle and respectable classes.* On several days during the election,

---

* The following satirical lines on the conduct of the mayor were published and freely circulated during the contest:

Mr. Stanley's committee, seeing that Mr. Hunt's friends had forcible possession of the booths, appealed for his worship's interference, but he declined to comply with the request. At the election of July, 1830, in accordance with an act passed in 1828, limiting the election to eight days, the Corn Exchange, where the election took place, was divided into ten voting booths, and each booth was apportioned to one of the ten districts into which, for parochial purposes, the town was divided.   This arrangement Mr. Nicholas Grimshaw, the mayor, refused to adopt at the present election, allowing the voters to poll at whichever booth they might choose, and there being thus a less check on fraudulent votes, large numbers were tendered and received.   It was abundantly proved that hundreds of non-residents voted for Mr. Hunt on the occasion, and in one case it was ascertained beyond doubt that a man from Blackburn, voted for Mr. Hunt 13 times! It would.

> " By many 'twas said, a few years ago,
>   That the d——l came up from the regions below !
> As he thought 'twould be better on earth to reside,
> He fix'd upon Preston, so fam'd for its pride.

> " And for many years this father of evil
>   I'y all was politely addressed as the d——l;
> But lately he play'd them a slippery trick,
> And he's now better known by the name of ' Old Nick.'

> " And so for a time, perhaps, 'twill continue :
> But Preston, oh! Preston! the d——l's still in you!
> 'Tis thought times will change, and the people grow civil.
> And ' Old Nick ' again, may return to the d——l."

perhaps, be idle to deny that, amidst the reckless disregard of order, and the saturnalia which prevailed, several fictitious votes were also given for Mr. Stanley, but that he was defeated mainly by non-resident voters has never been questioned. After seven days' voting the seat was given to Mr. Hunt, the numbers being—for Mr. Hunt, 3,730, and for Mr. Stanley, 3,392; the political connexion of the Stanley family with Preston, which had existed for so many years, being thus suddenly and unexpectedly severed. Satisfied of the undue influences which had been used against him, and of the illegal character of the voting, Mr. Stanley threatened to have a scrutiny of the votes at the close of the poll, before the return was made, the returning officer at that time having the power of deciding as to the validity of votes so objected to. Arrangements were made for this purpose, and Mr. Sergeant Mereweather came down to conduct it on behalf of Mr. Stanley, but, after three days' preparation, it was abandoned. The result was deeply mortifying to Mr. Stanley himself, and not less to the whole of the Knowsley family, who evinced their sense of the slight by withdrawing all their patronage and influence from the town, which severely felt the separation.* The

---

* The following lines were published and circulated after the election :—

> "Oh! Preston, Preston, once the proud,
> Hast thou not now proclaim'd aloud—
> In honour thou art lacking?

then Earl of Derby, twelfth Earl (and grandfather to the present Earl) who, as we have already stated, as well as the eleventh Earl and other members of the family, was born in Preston, keenly felt the blow, and in a short time after the close of the contest, the windows of Patton-house, in Church-street, the family mansion in Preston, were blocked up, and all the attendants withdrawn, giving to the otherwise noble building a desolate and dismal appearance; the races, also, which the family had warmly patronized, they no longer supported, which caused them to be discontinued, and generally the Stanleys withdrew themselves from all association with the town.

Mr. Stanley left Preston much chagrined and dispirited, having just been appointed to a highly responsible post in the new government, but now with-

> Reject the noble Stanley's son,
> And let thy choice be fix'd upon
>   A blackguard son of blacking!
>
> "Oh! Preston, Preston, shame to thee!
> Thou'st stamped thy name with infamy;
>   Thy glory is departed.
> Thy honour in the dust is laid!
> A bye-word and a scoff thou'rt made
>   By all that's noble-hearted.
>
> "Oh! Preston, not yet *quantum suf.*
> To make thyself quite black enough,
>   And prove that thou art barren!
> In all that's counted great and good,
> Thou'st only now to turn out Wood,
>   And bring in Robert Warren!"

out a seat in the House of Commons. His colleagues
in the new ministry, however, felt that the influence
of his powerful oratory was required, and must be
provided for in the coming debates on the Reform
Bill, and Sir Hussey Vivian, then member for Windsor,
gave up his seat in favour of Mr. Stanley, who was at
once returned for the royal borough.

In the debates which took place on the Reform
Bill, in 1831, Mr. Stanley, although not in the
cabinet, was one of the most powerful and influential
speakers in favour of the government measure; and
perhaps one of the most eloquent speeches which he
ever delivered in the course of his parliamentary
career, was that which he made on the evening of
Friday, the 4th of March, during the adjourned debate
on the second reading, when he answered, amongst
other members who had attacked the bill, the late
Sir Robert Peel, who had spoken the previous evening.
His irony and sarcasm were chiefly directed against
Sir Robert, whose speech he mercilessly analysed and
dissected. Almost at the outset of his remarks, he
said:—" I feel that I labour under extraordinary
" difficulties in addressing the House at the present
" moment, because I shall consider it my duty to call
" its attention to some portions of that commanding
" and powerful, I had almost said convincing speech,
" to which the House listened with so much attention
" at the conclusion of last night's debate; and, in the

"observations which I shall make upon the right
"honourable baronet's address, I trust it is unneces-
"sary for me to assure the right honourable gentle-
"man, as that right honourable gentleman has assured
"the noble lords and right honourable gentlemen on
"the ministerial side of the House, that I enter upon
"the discussion with no hostile or angry feelings
"towards the right honourable baronet, for there is
"no man in the House of whose talents, ability, and
"integrity, I have a higher opinion."

After expressing his regret that Sir Robert's
opinions on the question of Reform were so directly
opposed to those of his Majesty's ministers, he sarcas-
tically added, " I have, however, had the satisfaction
"of seeing the opinions of the right honourable baro-
"net gradually change on one great question, and
"should the present ministers succeed in this measure,
"I trust that an experience of its beneficial effects
"will reconcile the right honourable baronet to that
"which he now contemplates with a feeling of
"anxiety and disapprobation."   After taunting the
right honourable baronet with having stated that if
any danger or public disaffection should arise from
the failure of the measure, the responsibility must be
thrown on the shoulders of the ministry who had
brought it forward, and not on those who opposed it,
Mr. Stanley said, " I, however, will contend that the
"responsibility must rest with those on the other

"side of the House, who could not go on with the
"government, because they were disposed to resist
"all Reform.   If those gentlemen, who, in place,
"resisted all efficient Reform, and who went out
"because they would not agree to it, though it was
"loudly called for by the people—if they afterwards
"endeavour to baffle the efforts of those who have
"succeeded them—who are anxious for the success
"of a measure of Reform—if they strive to baffle and
"embarrass those who came in bound and pledged
"to Parliamentary Reform, then the right honourable
"baronet and his friends must take upon themselves
"the responsibility that will attach to the loss and
"defeat of the great measure.   But the right honour-
"able baronet says, 'Why has government brought it
"'forward?   It is a bad time, and it ought not to be
"'introduced now.'   In answer to this I ask, what
"was the conditional pledge upon which ministers
"came in, and without which my noble friend and
"right honourable friends near me would not have
"accepted office?   It was that we would bring for-
"ward a measure of Reform.   Now, with this pledge
"on our lips—with those principles in our hearts
"which we have always maintained, we entered office.
"We appeared as the friends of Parliamentary Re-
"form, hoping, as we yet do, to have the public feeling
"with us when we propose a measure on that subject,
"and what is the kind advice which, under these

"circumstances, the right honourable baronet gives
"us? He says, 'Now that you are in office, tell the
"'people that the time is not convenient for Reform.'
"If the ministers acted on such a principle as that,
"then, indeed, a fearful responsibility would rest
"upon their shoulders. Dreadful would be the con-
"sequences arising from disappointed hopes and high
"raised expectations blighted and falsified by the
"mean conduct of those upon whom the people had
"relied! Procrastination in these cases is always
"mischievous, and the late government might have
"learnt an important lesson from the consequences
"of delay in carrying the Catholic question." After
defending the Ministers and the Reform Bill for a
considerable length of time, amidst the breathless
attention of the House, Mr. Stanley in continuation
remarked, "But then, it is said that the measure is
"revolutionary. To this it is scarcely necessary for
"me to urge more in reply than a mere denial of any
"such object on the part of those who have intro-
"duced it. I may observe, however, that I am not
"likely to be a party to any measure of that kind.
"Is my noble friend, who introduced the measure to
" the House, a man without any stake in the country ?
"Is not the name he bears in itself a guarantee
"against any such intention ? Is my noble friend,
" the noble Earl at the head of the government—he
"who is said to be strenuously attached to the pri-

"vileges of his order—who has, on more than one
"occasion, been made the object of attack on that
"ground—is he, I repeat, likely to advocate a mea-
"sure which is to involve those privileges, and to
"involve the monarchy in one common ruin? Look
"around at the other members of his Majesty's
"government, and of those who have come forward
"to support them on this occasion, are they men of
"no fortune, mere adventurers, who would have
"everything to gain, and nothing to lose by a revo-
"lution? Or are they not men who have large
"stakes in the country, and whose individual interests
"are bound up with the permanent peace and security
"of the state? What, then, could they gain by the
"chance medley of a revolution?" The right
honourable gentleman concluded this celebrated and
powerful speech with the following brilliant peroration: "I earnestly implore honourable members, by
"their sense of justice to the country, by their respect
"to what is due to the people, by their regard for
"the maintenance of that glorious constitution which
"has been handed down to us by our ancestors—
"[great cheering on the Opposition side]—I repeat that
"constitution which ministers are now endeavouring,
"not to violate, but to amend,—by their regard for
"the permanency of our institutions, and the peace
"and security of the state,—I call on them by all
"these considerations, by their respect for the peti-

" tions of the people, for what may be lawfully asked,
" and cannot be constitutionally refused—to support
" his Majesty's ministers in their endeavours to
" uphold and cement the legitimate rights of the
" Crown, the aristocracy, and the people, and by so
" doing, to fix the whole, as well as their own fame,
" on the imperishable basis of the affections of the
" people." Mr. Stanley frequently spoke on the
measure afterwards, and finally wound up the several
protracted discussions which took place on the bill.

Upon Mr. Stanley devolved, as Chief Secretary
for Ireland, the duty of introducing into the House of
Commons the various measures connected with that
country, and unhappily at the time he took office, a
strong feeling of discontent existed there, which
manifested itself in open sedition. Disturbances and
rioting were of daily occurrence in several parts of the
country, and, repressive measures being necessary, the
" Irish Coercion Bill " was introduced into Parliament,
Mr. Stanley having the bill in charge. Mr. O'Connell,
who was at that time in the zenith of his power, and
held almost unchallenged sway over the great bulk of
the Irish people, was a deadly enemy to the government of which Mr. Stanley was a member. He was
in the habit of denouncing Earl Grey and his colleagues as the " base, bloody, and brutal whigs;" and
Mr. Stanley came under the especial lash of the arch
Irish agitator, his coercion bill being fiercely and

violently attacked by O'Connell, and Mr. Stanley himself being denounced in the House as "Scorpion Stanley;" but although "the Liberator" was so constantly singling out Mr. Stanley as his chief object of attack, he was often heard to say that there was no member of the House whose withering and eloquent satire he more felt than that of his antagonist. Notwithstanding the opposition of O'Connell, and those who acted with him, Mr. Stanley's firmness and powerful reasoning convinced the House that the measure, exceptional as it was, was necessary, and the Irish Coercion Bill became law. The passing of this measure increased —if indeed that were possible—the bitter feeling of hostility which Mr. O'Connell, Mr. Sheil, and other Irish members entertained towards Mr. Stanley, and from that period until the year 1833, when he resigned the office of Chief Secretary for Ireland and became Principal Secretary of State for the Colonies, he was unceasingly denounced as the greatest enemy of the sister country. But throughout the whole of the stormy debates which took place during the period, Mr. Stanley, by his perfect self-possession, his matchless powers as an orator and debater, and his withering sarcasm, proved himself more than equal to his antagonists, who, feeling themselves over-powered and vanquished by his extraordinary powers of invective, at length began to utter complaints to the House of the right hon. gentleman's intolerable

pride and hauteur, which elicited from Sir Robert
Peel a scornful and crushing reply, in the course of
which he said, "Often have I heard the right hon.
"gentleman taunted with his aristocratic demeanour.
"I rather think I should hear fewer complaints upon
"that score if he were a less powerful opponent in
"debate." The measures which Mr. Stanley was
instrumental in carrying for the amelioration of the
condition of Ireland, during the time he held the
office of Chief Secretary, are in themselves evidence
that the charges preferred against him by Mr. O'Connell
and others, were altogether undeserved, and prove
moreover, that his opponents at the time referred to,
both in and out of Parliament, had not studied
Ireland and her people so deeply and so closely as
at the period when he was Irish Secretary, Mr.
Stanley did; and as the following extract from the
British and Foreign Review, for April, 1837, bears
upon the class of objectors referred to, we give it
at length as an appropriate accompaniment to this part
of our sketch :—

"When," says the reviewer, "the Duke of Welling-
"ton and Sir Robert Peel yielded to necessity
"the measure of emancipation which they had
"denied to justice, they taught Ireland a lesson of
"agitation, which she put into immediate practice,
"and continues to use with increasing energy and
"dangerous efficiency to this hour.   The most stirring

"question that could address itself to the national
"passions, a Repeal of the Union with all its associa-
"tions of domestic independence was put forward.
"At this crisis Mr. Stanley was appointed Chief
"Secretary for Ireland. He had filled for a short
"time, some subordinate office in the Colonial
"department, most likely us a preparatory exercise
"for official business, and gave proof thus early of
"qualities which he has since more prominently
"displayed—diligence, dispatch, a promptitude of
"decision, all but precipitate, and a fearless self-
"reliance all but rash. He appeared to enter upon
"the duties of his office, as much from a love of labour
"as from political ambition, or a desire of fame. It
"was remarked by all persons who approached him
"during his official career, that when the data for
"forming an opinion were placed before him he saw
"their effect at a glance, however complicated or
"minute, and his conclusions were generally as just
"as they were rapid. It has been charged as a fault
"upon his practice as a minister, or in the constitution
"of his mind, that he applied himself over much to
"details, and would examine with his own eye the
"most minute points. Attention to particulars was
"not a fault but an advantage, to one whose con-
"clusions were so decisive, and those who imagine
"that this habit of mind is inconsistent with general
"principles and comprehensive views fall into a great

"error. Few men have been known to attain the
"exercise and the reputation of accomplished and
"superior talents in debate within so short a period.
"He manifested at the very outset not only the
"prompt facilities, but the severe task of a
"master of the art. The ambitious ornaments of
"rhetoric, the flights of imagination, and affectation
"of the figurative, that false brilliant which is so
"alluring to youthful orators, never for an instant
"dazzled the ill-judging, or offended the judicious, in
"his speeches. The vigour of his mind was only the
"more advantageously exhibited, from the unadorned
"simplicity of his language. His speeches on subjects
"on which he might naturally be supposed to come to
"the House prepared, have the air of being unpremedita-
"ted, while those produced at the call of the moment,
"from the felicity and force of his diction, and his
"instinctive facility of method and order in his topics
"and arguments, have the appearance of elaborate
"composition. As an opponent he is formidable and
"vigilant, quick to observe and dexterous to profit
"by an advantage; no one follows up success with
"more pitiless force, or embarrasses more effectually
"where he cannot distinctly refute; at the same time
"his oratory like his character is wholly free from
"the disingenuous and petty. He does not bring to
"his aid the graces of literature, or the more popular
"endowments of wit and pleasantry, but his reading

"is manifest wherever it is necessary to cite the
"events of history or the authority of the wise, and
"there is no one whose derision and sarcasm are at
"once more withering and polite. He does not
"affect the forms of logic, but has that better and
"less palpable art of reasoning which is called
"dialecticks, and exercises it with vigour and adroit-
"ness. It may be added, as action is an essential
"accomplishment in an orator, that his attitude is
"manly, free, and apparently unstudied or unthought
"of, his gestures impressive and graceful without art."

In 1832, on the elevation of his father to the
peerage, he succeeded him as representative for the
northern division of Lancashire. During the same
year his great talents as an orator and debater,
materially assisted in carrying the Reform Bill, and
in the same session of Parliament he had the satisfaction of introducing, and carrying successfully through
the legislature, the first great measure of National
Education for Ireland, which has been attended with
such advantageous results. In the session of 1833 he
also brought into Parliament and carried the Irish
Church Temporalities Bill, the effect of which was
to do away with certain abuses connected with the
revenues of the church, and to place them upon a
more equitable footing; and which had also the effect
of reducing the number of Irish bishops. With the
passing of this measure his connexion with Ireland in

an official capacity ceased, and he accepted the office
of Secretary of State for the Colonies, thus for the first
time becoming a Cabinet Minister.

Almost his first step, if indeed it was not actually
his first, after entering the cabinet, was to introduce
a bill providing for the emancipation of the West
Indian slaves, a measure of the gravest importance
to the West Indian planters, and not only so, but
what was of still greater consequence, when viewed
in its moral and social aspect, it aimed at wiping out
the disgrace which had hitherto attached to this
country, that of permitting, if not encouraging the
traffic in human flesh.   The bill was introduced on
the 14th of May, 1833, and after being carefully
discussed and considered it finally received the
sanction of Parliament.   Mr. Stanley, in introducing
the bill, made one of the most eloquent and effective
speeches ever delivered within the walls of Parliament.
In the course of this splendid oration the right hon.
gentlemen said :—

   " The present question involves interests greater,
" consequences more momentous, results more porten-
" tous, than any which were ever submitted to the
" British or other legislature.   A commerce giving
" employment now to 250,000 tons of shipping, a
" revenue of £500,000, and an export of equal amount,
" is here to be dealt with.   But what are these
" pecuniary interests, great as they are, to the moral

" and social consequences at stake, the freedom of
" 800,000 of our own, and many millions of foreign
" slaves; the emancipation and happiness of generations
" yet unborn ; the ultimate destiny of almost a moiety
" of the human race, which is wound up with this
" question ? Vast, almost awful as are the interests
" involved in this question, and the difficulties with
" which it is beset, its settlement can no longer be
" delayed. We have arrived at a point where delay
" is more perilous than decision. We have only the
" choice left of doing some good at the least risk of
" effecting evil. We are called upon to legislate
" between conflicting parties, one deeply interested by
" pecuniary interests, and by difficulties ever pressing
" and still increasing ; the other still more deeply
" interested by their feelings and opinions, and
" representing a growing determination on the part of
" the people of this country, at once to put an end to
" slavery ; a determination the more absolute and the
" less irresistible, that it is founded in sincere
" religious feelings, and in a solemn conviction that
" things wrong in principle cannot be expedient in
" practice. The time is gone by when the question
" can for a moment be entertained whether or not
" the system of slavery can be made perpetual ; the
" only point left for discussion is the safest, happiest
" way of effecting its entire abolition."

But, although Mr. Stanley had thus been associated with the Whigs in passing some of the most important liberal and constitutional measures which were ever introduced into Parliament, the Reform Bill being the chief, his connexion with the great Whig party was now about to terminate.   Events occurred between the close of the session of 1833 and the commencement of that of 1834, which were destined to cause a separation between Mr. Stanley and his colleagues. He had already, as we have seen, brought in and carried the Irish Church Temporalities Bill, and so far as the disposal of the revenues of the Irish Church were concerned, he did not think they ought to be further disturbed.   But, in the early part of the session of 1834, it was proposed in the cabinet again to interfere with the Irish Church establishment, by diminishing still further its revenues.   Accordingly it was understood that the " Irish Church Appropriation Bill " was introduced into the cabinet, whereupon Mr. Stanley declined to be a party to the measure, and, in consequence of its having been brought forward, he seceded from the government, resigning his office as Colonial Secretary, and being accompanied in his retirement from the ministry by Sir James Graham, first Lord of the Admiralty; the Earl of Ripon, Lord Privy Seal; and the Duke of Richmond, Postmaster-General.   On the retirement of Mr. Stanley and his colleagues, O'Connell caused much amusement and laughter in the house by quoting from

Canning's well known " Loves of the Triangles," which appeared in the pages of the *Anti-Jacobin*, the lines :—

> " Still down thy steep, romantic Ashbourne, glides
> " The Derby Dilly with its six insides."

On Monday, the 2nd of June, 1834, a few days after his secession from the ministry, Mr. Stanley spoke warmly, and.at great length, against the proposal Mr. Ward, the member for St. Albans, had brought forward, a motion to the effect that as the amount of church property in Ireland was beyond the wants and requirements of the Protestant Church establishment, the Irish Church revenues should be reduced, and the money appropriated to the purposes of general education.   Lord Althorp, who was Chancellor of the Exchequer at the time, on the evening of the 2nd of June, when the adjourned debate on Mr. Ward's motion came on, stated that the King, by the advice of his ministers, had appointed a commission of enquiry into the state of church property, and church affairs generally in Ireland, with the view among other things, of ascertaining the relative numbers of Protestants, Roman Catholics, and Dissenters in the several parishes ; and the noble Lord stated, in the course of his remarks, that it was the intention of the government to act upon the report of that commission. He concluded by moving, as an amendment to Mr. Ward's motion, the previous question.   Mr. Stanley followed in an oration of great power and fervour, and concluded a speech against both the motion and the appointment of the commission, with the following splendid peroration :—

"Let me call upon you to pause before you assent to a "resolution which you cannot, which you ought not, "which the people of England will not let you, carry into "effect. I did not think I should ever live to hear a "minister of the crown propose such a resolution : I do "not think that I shall yet live to see a legislature which "will pass it; and I am not certain that I know the sove-"reign who will give his assent to it even if it be passed. "I have honestly and conscientiously gone the full length "to which I am prepared to go in reforming the abuses of "the Church,—I say the abuses of the Church, for I "admit there are questions regarding pluralities, regarding "non-residence, regarding the internal discipline of the "Church, regarding its purification and amendment, re-"garding the increased respectability of its ministers, and "regarding the better distribution of its revenues for "Church purposes, to which we are bound to give imme-"diate attention ; but the question of the appropriation of "the property of the Church to any other but Church "purposes involves principles to which I, for one, can "never give my assent. In concert with no man save "those noble and honourable individuals who have acted "upon the principles which I have just explained to the "House, pursuing the course which my own sense of "honour and public duty points out to me ; desirous of

" cautioning the House not to assent to an abstract resolu-
" tion of this nature, without knowing at what time, by
" what means, and by what men it is to be carried into
" effect ; prepared on my own behalf to put a decided
" negative upon it, yet prevented from doing so by the
" reasons which I have already stated ; anxious not to
" draw down upon myself, and upon those who have on
" this occasion acted with me, the responsibility of endan-
" gering, by taking a different course than that marked
" out by the government, the passing of that amendment
" which all parties in the House seem equally to deprecate ;
" desirous, 1 repeat, of not seeing this resolution carried
" into effect ; confident that, without danger to both
" countries, it cannot be carried into effect, I am compelled
" to agree to the amendment of my noble friend, the
" previous question."

It has already been shewn that on Irish questions
especially there had always been a bitter spirit of
antagonism displayed between Mr. Stanley and Mr.
O'Connell, but upon the present occasion, the latter
generously admitted the perfect sincerity of the right
honourable gentleman ; for, in a speech delivered
almost immediately after Mr. Stanley had resumed
his seat, he said, adverting to the right honourable
gentleman's resignation :—

" I think his policy most erroneous ; I think he
" has pursued a course of most pernicious measures
" to my country.   I think he has swamped the govern-

"ment on its commencement; but I see in him an
"inflexible integrity of purpose; I behold him
"faithful and true to his principles, bold and manly
"in the avowal of his opinions, able and eloquent in
"the vindication of them, high in his sense of honour,
"and firm, indeed, and disinterested in the assertion
"of that which he thinks to be the sacred duty of
"conscience."

The commission announced by Lord Althorp
was not carried out, for the government, which had
been reconstructed, with Lord Melbourne at its head,
Earl Grey having resigned, went out of office in
November, and was succeeded by a ministry with
Sir Robert Peel at its head, the Duke of Wellington
holding the reins of government temporarily for
three weeks, until the arrival home from the
Continent of Sir Robert Peel. Mr. Stanley was
invited by Sir Robert to join the government, but he
declined to do so. The Peel ministry, however, only
existed for about three months, Sir Robert throwing
up the reins of government in April, 1835, after
being defeated at the general election which followed
upon his acceptance of office. Lord Melbourne was thus
again called to the helm, and the Whigs were in the
ascendant from 1835 to 1841, when they were
defeated on the budget, Mr. Stanley who had for several
years acted with the Conservative party, having
spoken against the budget, which he attacked in one

of those withering speeches for which he had now become celebrated and famous.

On the defeat and resignation of Lord Melbourne's administration in 1841, Sir Robert Peel was again called in, and on the 3rd of September he formed his second administration, Mr. Stanley joining the new government as Secretary of State for the Colonies, the same office which he had already filled in the ministry of Earl Grey. It was during Sir Robert's administration, namely, in 1844, that Mr. Stanley was summoned to the House of Peers under his father's barony, as Lord Stanley of Bickerstaffe, and from that period to the present his lordship has undoubtedly been accepted as the Conservative leader in the upper chamber of the legislature. The Peel administration, led in the Commons by the Premier, and in the Peers by Lord Stanley, was for many years a strong and vigorous government, with a powerful majority in the House of Commons, the Premier and Lord Stanley working harmoniously together; but in 1845, Sir Robert, who had hitherto been a Protectionist, declared his conversion to the principles of free trade, and this ultimately led to a separation between the Premier and Lord Stanley, the latter steadfastly adhering to those Protectionist principles which he had uniformly and consistently held. In December, 1845, at Christmas, Sir Robert Peel resigned the seals of office, and Lord John Russell

knowing that he himself was in a minority in the
House, advised the Queen to send for Lord Stanley as
the leader of the Protectionist party, but his lordship
declined, on which Lord John Russell, then in a
minority in the Commons, undertook the duty of
forming a ministry, which, however, only existed for
three weeks.   On the dissolution of Lord John
Russell's government, Sir Robert Peel was again sent
for, and at the commencement of 1846 re-constructed
his government on the avowed principles of free
trade, and a repeal of the Corn Laws.   Lord Stanley,
firm to his Protectionist principles, did not return to
office, but in conjunction with Mr. Disraeli and the
late Lord George Bentinck, resolutely opposed the
free trade policy of the Premier in those memorable
debates which preceded the repeal of the Corn Laws.
The final result of this great struggle is easily told—
the Corn Laws were repealed, and the principles of
free trade from that moment prevailed, the Premier
openly and candidly declaring to the House that the
issue was entirely due to " the unadorned eloquence
of Richard Cobden."

After the passing of the act repealing the Corn
Laws, Sir Robert Peel, in the summer of 1846, threw
up the seals of office, and a Whig government,
presided over by Lord John Russell, once more
ruled the destinies of the country, extending over
five years, from 1846 to 1852.   During the whole of

this period Lord Stanley was at the head of the
Conservative Opposition, and in the course of those
years he displayed his fine oratorical abilities in
several speeches which he made on the question
of the Irish Poor Laws, and other subjects
affecting Ireland, including the deplorable affair at
Dolly's Brae; together with an eloquent and ex-
haustive speech on the complications which at
that time existed in Greece. In 1851 Lord Stanley
was again offered the Premiership, Lord John
Russell's government having resigned in consequence
of their unexpected defeat in February of that year, by
a majority of forty-eight, on Mr. Locke King's motion
for an extention of the county franchise. For a second
time Lord Stanley declined the proffered honour,
and gave his reasons for doing so in his place in the
House of Lords, on Friday, 28th of February. On
Lord Stanley thus refusing to take the reins of
Government, Lord John Russell returned to his post,
and remained Premier until 1852. On the 20th of February in that year, Lord Palmerston moved an amendment on the Militia Bill brought forward by the government, which was carried, and the ministry resigned.

Lord Derby—for he had then succeeded to the
earldom, his father having died in June, 1851—was
now, for the third time, solicited to form an administration, when he accepted the task, and having completed his arrangements and formed his government,

he made his first ministerial statement in the House
of Lords, on the 27th of February, concluding in the
following eloquent and characteristic terms :—" Be the
" period of my administration longer or shorter, not
" only shall I have attained the highest object of my
" ambition, but I shall have fulfilled one of the highest
" ends of human being, if, in the course of that admin-
" istration, I can in the slightest degree advance the
" great object of peace on earth and good-will among
" men ; if I can advance the social, moral, and reli-
" gious improvement of my country, and, at the same
" time, contribute to the safety, honour, and welfare of
" our sovereign and her dominions."   The majority of
the House of Commons, at the time of Lord Derby's
advent to office, was decidedly hostile to a Conservative government, and, therefore little beyond routine
business took place during the following spring and
summer, the Premier having determined to dissolve
the Parliament and test the feeling of the country.
The dissolution took place on the 1st of July, and the
result of the general election was adverse to the
government, which was shortly afterwards shewn on
the assembling of the new Parliament. On the 16th of
December in the same year, the ministry was defeated
on their budget, after four nights' discussion, by a
majority of nineteen, on which Lord Derby instantly
placed his resignation in the hands of her Majesty,
which was at once accepted.

On the resignation of the Earl of Derby, the Earl of Aberdeen, at the head of the "ministry of all talents," as it was somewhat satirically called, succeeded to office, but breaking down in the following year—1853, the Earl of Derby was a fourth time sent for by her Majesty, but declined to resume office on the very reasonable plea that the majority of the House of Commons was antagonistic to him. Lord Palmerston then succeeded to the premiership, which he retained until 1858, when he was defeated by an adverse vote of nineteen, on the conspiracy Bill, and his policy towards France. It is a most remarkable circumstance, and altogether without a parallel, that three governments in succession should have been defeated by the same numerical majority, and two of them on the same day and month in the year. Lord John Russell's government was beaten on the 20th of February, 1852, by a majority of nineteen; the Earl of Derby's first ministry was defeated on the 16th of December in the same year, by a majority of nineteen; and on the 20th of February, 1858, Lord Palmerston's government was overthrown on his French policy, by the ominous majority of nineteen; a conjunction of events which, as we have already stated, is unparalleled in history.

On the downfall of the Palmerston administration, the Earl of Derby was again entrusted with the formation of a ministry, which he quickly effected; assum-

ing, for the second time, the dignified and responsible
duties of Premier. And it is an interesting circumstance in connexion with the construction of Lord
Derby's second administration that he selected his
own son to fill one of the most important offices in the
cabinet. There may be some sufficiently hypercritical
to object to such an appointment on the ground of its
savouring of nepotism, but the contention involves a
fallacy which is essentially groundless. The appointment met with the universal approval of the entire
community, and it would have been the most trans-
parent affectation on the part of the Premier to have
ignored what everybody cordially believed, the pre-
eminent fitness of his son to be the new Premier's
Indian Chief Secretary. The new ministry had no
sooner been installed in office, than the Premier and
his colleagues entered upon the duties of sound practical legislation, and one of its first and most important
acts was the complete re-organization and consolidation
of the Indian government, under the immediate direction of the noble Lord to whom that department of
the cabinet had been entrusted, and whose personal residence in India for a considerable period, had rendered
him peculiarly fitted for carrying those desired reforms
which were by all admitted to be necessary in the
management of our Indian affairs. Several other
important enactments were carried out in the early
months of the government of 1858, not the least im-

portant of which was the admission of the Jews into
Parliament. The session of 1858 having closed, the
cabinet, during the recess, prepared a measure of Parliamentary Reform, a question which had for a lengthened
period occupied the time and attention of successive
governments, but which none had yet been able to
settle. Shortly after the meeting of Parliament for
the session of 1859, the government brought in a bill
for the reform of Parliament, of an exceedingly comprehensive character. Had that bill been successfully
carried through the House it would have conferred the
elective franchise on a very considerable number of
intelligent persons who did not then possess it, but
when the bill came to be discussed, it encountered
the fiercest opposition from different quarters. It was
objected to and denounced on several grounds, one of
which—a favourite one with Mr. Disraeli, its author—
was the "fancy franchises," and ultimately the government were once more baffled in their endeavours
to settle the question which for years had stood in the
way of all practical legislation. They were defeated
on the second reading of the bill on the 31st of
March, by a majority of 39, when, in accordance with
the advice of her ministers, the Queen dissolved
Parliament on the 23rd of April, the prorogation
having taken place on the Tuesday previous, April
19th.

After the general election which followed the

dissolution, the new Parliament assembled on the 31st of May, and the Right Hon. John Evelyn Denison having been unanimously again elected Speaker, the swearing in of members proceeded, and occupied several days.   On the 7th of June her Majesty in person opened the new Parliament, and the same evening the discussion on the address in answer to her Majesty's speech, took place in both Houses.   In the House of Lords the address was unanimously agreed to, but in the House of Commons an amendment was proposed by the Marquis of Hartington, member for North Lancashire, to the effect that her Majesty's ministers did not possess the confidence of the House and the country.   The amendment was seconded by Mr. Hanbury, member for Middlesex.   The debate extended to four nights, and on the 10th of June the amendment was carried in a very full house, by a majority of 13, the numbers being 323 for it, and 310 against it.   On the following day both Houses adjourned to Friday, June 17th, and on that day the Earl of Derby in the House of Lords, and Mr. Disraeli in the House of Commons, announced the resignation of ministers, in consequence of the adverse vote which had been arrived at.

In the autumn of 1859, namely, on Saturday, the 29th of October, a splendid banquet was given to the Earl of Derby and his colleagues, in the Philharmonic Hall, at Liverpool, when the noble Earl and

every member of his late Cabinet, except General
Peel, were present. The attendance was large and
influential, and the reception of the ex-Premier and
his late ministers was cordial and enthusiastic,
amounting to nothing less than a great ovation.
During the proceedings, the following address, signed
by 7090 of the principal inhabitants, was presented
to his lordship :—

"To the Right Hon. the Earl of Derby, K.G.

"We, the undersigned inhabitants of the borough of
"Liverpool, desire to approach your lordship with pro-
"found sentiments of respect and gratitude for the
"services you have so loyally rendered to the crown
"and country during a period of unexampled difficulty;
"and to congratulate your lordship on the distinguished
"honour with which her Majesty, by investing you
"with the Order of the Garter, has this day graced your
"retirement from office.

"The crisis at which your lordship was called upon
"to assume the duties of the Premiership was one of
"deep anxiety.

"There was then, both in France and England, a
"feeling of irritated nationality, which threatened to sever
"the friendship so necessary to their mutual prosperity.

"The slightest error in diplomacy might have kindled
"among noble and generous allies, the feuds and enmities
"of ancient days.

"Your firmness and prudence were found equal to

"the occasion. By your wise counsels the jealous suscepti-
"bilities of both countries were honourably satisfied.

"The despatches on foreign affairs recently published,
"prove the earnest and wise endeavours of your govern-
"ment to maintain the peace of the world, while they
"show how sincere were your efforts to promote real freedom
"in Italy.

"We recognise in these despatches not only the
"greatest talent, but a firm and dignified spirit, and a
"sound English feeling.

"Your country gratefully acknowledges that at this
"trying period, when great nations have been stirred by
"passions which threaten the peace of the whole world,
"your government has avoided all entangling alliances,
"has maintained the strictest neutrality, and has placed
"the defences of England on a basis of powerful security.

"History will regard your administration as a bright
"page in our country's annals; for therein is written
"'India pacified,' 'Our army victorious,' and 'Our navy
"'unprecedentedly powerful.'

"The difficulties of your position were increased by
"the necessity of acting with an adverse House of
"Commons; and thus many of your legislative measures,
"though based on justice, and calculated to meet the
"wants of the country, were met by opposing majorities.

"It is painful to reflect that party spirit overrules
"every motive of action among unpatriotic legislators,
"and that from the subdivisions of political parties the
"Queen's government is dependent for the success of

"measures on the caprices of small, intriguing, and "restless sections—themselves irresponsible, and, therefore, "indifferent to consequences.

"By a combination of those sections the country has "been deprived of your lordship's services, but happily "not before your measures had proved the policy of your "government to have been based on constitutional progress "and the advancement of material prosperity."

This address, which was beautifully engrossed on vellum, was enclosed in a superb silver casket, the arms of Liverpool, and also the Derby arms, being on the shield, inside the lid, and underneath was the following inscription:—"This Casket, containing an "Address, signed by 7090 Conservatives of Liverpool, "was presented to the Right Hon. the Earl of Derby, "K.G., 29th October, 1859. The presentation was "followed by a banquet at the Philharmonic Hall, "Francis Shand, Esq., in the Chair."

In replying to the toast of his health, at the banquet, in the evening, the Earl of Derby delivered a long and interesting speech, which was throughout characterized by that power and eloquence of which his lordship is so great a master. In the course of his speech, the noble Earl dwelt at considerable length, in explanation of those principles of Conservatism, upon which he and his colleagues had always acted. Stating what he believed true Conservatism to be, he said :—

"I mean by this, not that Conservatism, falsely
"so called, which would obstruct all useful change;
"but I would speak of that Conservatism which is
"not obstruction, and which is the best promoter of
"safe and gradual social improvement—of that Con-
"servatism which, strenuously adhering to the old
"machinery of the constitution, adapts, from time to
"time, the various parts of its mechanism to the real
"requirements and the real capacities of the age in
"which we live—of that Conservatism which should
"give to all orders and degrees of men within this
"realm their due weight, authority, and preponderance
"—of that Conservatism which loves the interests
"of the people at large, but will not be led away by
"the noisy demonstrations of blustering demagogues,
"either to shrink at the voice of menace, or timidly
"to concede rights and positions to large bodies of
"men, for the purpose of obtaining a temporary
"moment of popularity, when, in our hearts, we
"believe that the concession of those coveted boons
"would be the worst injury to the classes to whom
"we give them. Gentlemen, this is the Conservatism
"to which, I take it, you pledge yourselves by your
"attendance this day. They are the principles which
"I have ever professed, and upon which I have ever
"endeavoured to act." His lordship's allusion to the
late Sir Robert Peel, and the reasons why, in 1846,
he separated from the honourable baronet, and be-

came himself the leader of the Conservative party,
possess more than ordinary interest. " I wish," said
the noble Earl, " to speak in this assembly—as I
" have spoken upon all occasions—in no terms indi-
" cative of anything but the highest respect for the
" distinguished genius, and for the personal character
" of that great statesman, whom England has lately
" had to lament, the late Sir Robert Peel, and if there
" were any occasion upon which I could not speak in
" terms other than those which I have always used,
" it would be at a time when a melancholy domestic
" calamity has prevented the attendance of his nearest
" relation (General Peel), one of my most valued col-
" leagues in the late government, and who gave
" me most able and admirable assistance in the
" management of the most difficult department,
" namely, the civil department of the army in this
" country. But, gentlemen, I am not speaking dis-
" respectfully of the memory of a statesman with
" whom I had the honour of many years' personal
" friendship, and, I believe, reciprocal esteem, if I say
" that the course which, at the close of 1847, was
" taken by the late Sir Robert Peel, completely and
" entirely, for the moment, shattered the Conservative
" party in this country. Upon the failure of Lord
" John Russell's endeavour to form a government,
" I wrote confidentially to the most eminent
" man of the country—to the late Duke of Wel-

"lington—a warm and cordial admirer and sup-
"porter of Sir Robert Peel, and a man who
"had stood for many, many years prominent—the
"foremost man in the world in the eyes of his
"countrymen—I wrote to consult him as to the
"position of the Conservative party, and the best
"means of restoring that unity which had been so
"lamentably dissevered.   I received a long letter
"from the Duke of Wellington, which I need hardly
"say I have kept and deeply value, in which he
"explained to me his own position, and in which
"he stated, that having accepted, under the abortive
"attempt of Lord John Russell to form a govern-
"ment, the duties of the neutral position of Com-
"mander-in-chief of her Majesty's forces, he con-
"sidered that he had for ever broken off his
"political connection with any party.   He inti-
"mated his concurrence in the opinion which I
"had ventured to express, that the alienation of
"the Conservative party from Sir Robert Peel was
"not a mere temporary feeling, but that it was
"impossible that he should ever again place himself
"at their head with a prospect of success; and the
"Duke of Wellington, I will not say entreated, but
"I will say he exhorted me, as a matter of duty to
"my Sovereign and to my country, to throw aside
"all doubts and all hesitation, and to assume at once
"the leadership of that great Conservative party

"whose existence, and whose power he deemed to be
"essential to the well being of the country and all
"its institutions, and he almost implored me, in my
"attempt to form an administration, not to be dis-
"couraged by any difficulties, except those which
"should be absolutely insuperable, but to sacrifice all
"other feelings to the desire of serving my Sovereign.
"Gentlemen, for fourteen years I have endeavoured
"to act in the spirit of that wise and patriotic advice
"coming from that eminent man, and I have been
"rewarded by seeing the Conservative party, not only
"in Parliament, increasing in numbers and in union,
"but spreading their roots deeply into the feelings
"and the heart of the country, and forming, as our
"opponents are compelled to acknowledge,—and in
"doing so their fears rather magnify the position,—
"and declare that we are actually at this moment at
"the head of a Parliamentary majority."

On the resignation of the Earl of Derby's second
administration, Lord Palmerston once more assumed
the reins of power, which he held up to the time of his
death in 1865. The Earl of Derby continued during the
whole of that period, as he does down to the present
time, the recognised and brilliant leader of the
Conservative party, and during the discussion of the
various questions, which from time to time came
under consideration, his lordship invariably took a
prominent part, his opinions and advocacy being

looked up to with the greatest respect, and his
arguments and reasoning always powerful and
convincing. We may here observe that during Lord
Palmerston's premiership, the question of Reform,
so far as the cabinet was concerned, was allowed to
a great extent to sleep, for although it was well
understood that several of his colleagues were known
to be favourable to the subject being again introduced
into Parliament, the Premier himself regarded it as
a "bore," and the very mention of it was distasteful
to him. On his death, however, when Earl Russell
succeeded him at the head of the government, the
question was revived in the cabinet, and the Queen's
speech, at the opening of Parliament in 1866,
announced that a Reform Bill would be introduced
in the course of the session. In a week or two after
the opening of the session this promise was redeemed,
Mr. Gladstone, the Chancellor of the Exchequer,
bringing in a bill, the main features of which were a
£7 rental qualification in boroughs, and a £12 rental
qualification in counties, with the entire abolition
of the rating clause, as it existed under the act of 1832.
The proposal for the abolition of rating as a condition
for exercising the elective franchise, was strongly
opposed by the Conservative party, with the Earl of
Derby at their head, and the Conservatives being
assisted by a number of members from the Liberal
ranks, who were designated by Mr. Bright "the cave

of Adullam," and who have since been known by the title of "Adullamites;" the ministry were defeated, and thereupon at once resigned office.

The events which followed the resignation of Earl Russell's government after their defeat on the Reform Bill in 1866, are too recent to require any lengthened notice here, inasmuch as they must be fresh in the recollection of every one. Suffice it to say that the Earl of Derby was again sent for by the Queen, and for the third time undertook the task of forming an administration, and it is only due to his lordship here to say that seeing the state of public feeling and opinion on the subject of Reform—how equally parties were balanced, and how desirable it was that the question of Reform should be settled, his lordship made overtures to several of the leading members of the Liberal party to join his ministry, but they one and all firmly refused, and he was therefore reduced to the necessity of forming an administration composed exclusively of the members of his own party. In a few days he accomplished the undertaking; and when he made his first statement in the House of Lords as the new Premier, he informed the House of what had been his intention and wish as to the composition of his government. No legislation deserving of any special notice took place in 1866, for the session was far advanced, and with the defeat of the late government in the latter part of

the summer, there was little left but routine matters
to get through, and the session was brought to a close
at the usual period in August.

During the recess, speculation was rife as to what
ministers would do in the coming session on the
all-absorbing subject of Reform. Some people pre-
dicted that it would form no part of the ministerial
programme, in the speech to be delivered from the
throne, whilst, on the other hand, the great majority
of the public inclined to the belief that government
would not, by shelving it, trifle with a question which
had become a source of irritation and discontent, and
which, on several grounds, it was desirable should be
finally and effectually disposed of. Perhaps, when
Parliament rose at the close of the session of 1866,
ministers were quite as much in the dark as to their
own intentions as the world outside the Cabinet.
The probability is, that in the interval which prevailed during the recess, the government took advantage of the generally expressed wish throughout the country, that a resolute effort should be
made to dispose of the subject; and, at an early
period in their Cabinet councils, determined upon
submitting a proposal to Parliament, with the *bona
fide* intention of setting the matter at rest by an act
which should meet the approval of all parties, and,
accordingly, the subject of a reform bill having been
affirmatively named in the speech from the throne,

on the opening of the session of 1867, the Chancellor
of the Exchequer, during the following week, introduced a series of resolutions to the House, which we
may at once say were regarded with disfavour, and
which the Chancellor prudently withdrew, with as
little delay as decency and propriety would permit.
After repeated discussions, a bill was brought in
providing for a £6 rate paying franchise in towns,
and a £14 franchise in counties, which met with
considerable opposition. The discussion of the question is of too recent date to render it at all necessary
for us to dwell upon it in detail here. Mr. Disraeli
ultimately withdrew his first bill, and the world was
astonished by a Conservative government introducing
the most democratic measure of parliamentary reform
that was ever submitted to the legislature—household borough suffrage, subject to payment of rates,
and a £15 county franchise. This comprehensive
proposal completely "took the wind out of the sails"
of the more advanced Liberal party, whilst it stag-
gered many of the adherents of the government, and
three Members of the Cabinet—General Peel, Lord
Cranbourne, and the Earl of Carnarvon — fiercely
denounced the Premier and the Chancellor of the
Exchequer as having betrayed the party, and seceded
from the ministry in disgust. Mr. Disraeli, however,
managed, by that adroitness which he possesses in
such an eminent degree, not only to keep his own

party together, united in support of the Bill, but also to secure the co-operation of a very considerable number of the members of the Liberal party, and the measure had not been long in committee before it was made perfectly manifest that it was "safe." Several minor alterations were made, and a variety of amendments carried, but the Bill came out of committee with its main principle ratified, and Mr. Disraeli, the leader of the Conservative party, had the gratification and credit of carrying a Reform Bill through the House of Commons, more democratic in its character and provisions than any measure of a similar kind ever submitted by even the most advanced Liberal minister. When the Bill was carried to the House of Lords, very few obstacles to its passing presented themselves. The Earl of Derby candidly admitted that he had always been of opinion, that if we were to have an extension of the franchise there was nothing left for it but household suffrage, and the Peers, as a body, tacitly, at least, endorsed the sentiment by dealing tenderly with the measure, and allowing it to emerge from committee without any one of its main provisions having been altered or impaired. The rest may be told in a few words. The Bill unanimously passed the third reading, and received the royal assent; and the Earl of Derby, who, as Mr. Stanley, had much of the credit of passing the Reform Bill of 1832, introduced by the

Whig ministry, under Earl Grey, and which, at the time, was considered to be extremely liberal, has now, thirty-five years afterwards, he himself being Premier, succeeded in placing upon the statute book a measure, in comparison with which, the act of 1832 is of an essentially disfranchising character.

We have thus brought the parliamentary and political life of the Earl of Derby down to the session ending August, 1867, a session which, from the magnitude of the great measure carried during its sittings, will mark one of the most important epochs in the political history of this country, and be remembered as a period, when, under the guidance and advice of a Conservative Prime Minister, and one of the most talented and distinguished statesmen who ever presided over the destinies of a nation, the people of England had conferred upon them political privileges to an extent which they never before enjoyed.

As regards the political career of the Earl of Derby, it would be uncandid not to admit that he deserted the party with whom, in early life, he was so closely allied, and gradually seceded from the Whigs, until he has attained the dignified and prominent position which he now occupies, but an examination into the circumstances and facts in connexion with his first secession from the Whig government, in 1834, and for which he was virulently assailed and charged with inconsistency, must satisfy any unprejudiced enquirer, that his alleged inconsistency is rather ideal than real. It will be remembered, that it was on the question of the Appropriation of the Revenues of the Irish Church to other than Church purposes, that he threw up his office as Colonial Secretary, under Earl Grey, in the year above named, but it must be borne in mind that for many years before 1834, he had on repeated occasions expressed himself in strong terms against the Irish Church Revenues being so diverted, more especially in May, 1824, when Mr. Haine brought forward a motion on the Irish Church Establishment, which was warmly opposed by the then Mr. Stanley; and, in addition to the above named fact, Mr. Stanley, when he carried the Irish Church Temporalities Bill, in 1833, expressed his wish and desire that it would settle the Irish Church Question, and that there would be no further interference with its revenues. His secession, therefore, from the Whig government, on the occasion referred to, was consistent rather than the reverse, and by no means justified the bitter and malignant attacks which were made upon him at the time, and often repeated since. He has also been often accused of inconsistency in opposing the repeal of the Corn Laws, a charge so transparently groundless, inasmuch as he was always an avowed protectionist, that it is only necessary to draw attention to the charge in order to expose its folly. The real truth is, that the

Earl of Derby, like many other distinguished public
men in the present day, finds himself separated from
those with whom he was associated in earlier life, as
much from divergence or change of opinion on the
part of others as himself. There are many living
instances to which we could point in illustration of
our statement, but it is unnecessary to do so. It is
sufficient for us to believe that in every case to which
we allude, the individuals in question are actuated
by true patriotism, and a desire for their country's
welfare, and so with the Earl of Derby, whatever
other failings he may have,—as his detractors say,
he may be "impetuous and passionate," "rash and
despotic," "ready to exasperate," or "haughty and
aristocratic,"—and, as regards the latter accusation,
if, indeed, it be true, it need excite no wonder or
surprise, for "we do not expect the high-mettled
racer to herd with donkeys or snuff the ground,"—he
may or may not be obnoxious to any of these polite
appellatives, but leaving the decision of this point to
others, we do not hesitate to say that a more high
souled, single minded statesman, or one more sincerely devoted to the true interests of his Sovereign
and his country, never crossed the threshold of the
English Parliament. By jealous and envious minds
his oratory and debating powers have been depre-
ciated as being nothing more than "showy," but
those who know him best have spoken otherwise,

and it is appropriately remarked by Mr. Rochester,
that "as an orator, his reputation stands almost (in
"some particulars, altogether) unrivalled among his
"contemporaries: far beyond which, however, it should
"be added, that he has perhaps never in all the past,
"had any superior among the most gifted debaters in
"Parliament. In many of the subtler devices of ora-
"tory, he has long been recognized as an exquisite
"proficient, while to an acquired, but perfected mas-
"tery of that art of arts, he has brought those manifest
"natural endowments which are so essential to com-
"plete the influence, the charm, the glamour of the ac-
"complished rhetorician. Not that his diction is ever
"ornate, being at all times, indeed, superb in its
"graceful simplicity, but that in the very terseness
"and lucidity of his 'silver style' there are witcheries
"of sound far beyond the reach of mere verbal adorn-
"ment. His language, in truth, is always as devoid
"of ornament as it is replete with a nameless and
"irresistible fascination. It is to the manly purity
"and strength of his Saxon English that he owes
"much of his extraordinary power in discussion—the
"vital force of one surpassed by few as an orator, by
"none as a debater." And Lord Macaulay, speaking of
the Earl's knowledge of the science of parliamentary
defence and attack, says that "it resembles rather an
"instinct than an acquisition; and he alone, among all
"our great senatorial reputations, seems to have made

" himself, upon the instant, as it were, master of his
" art, instead of affecting this—as in other instances
" —slowly, and 'at the expense of an audience.'"
It was Sir Edward Bulwer Lytton who gave to the
Earl the distinguished and expressive title "the
Rupert of debate." In 1846, Sir Edward published a poem (which had previously appeared piece-
meal), entitled "The New Timon," comprising portraits of the most distinguished political chiefs of the
day, Lord Stanley, then leader of the Opposition,
being amongst them, and the following lines are ex-
tracted from the portraiture of his lordship :—

" One after one the lords of time advance ;
Here Stanley meets—here Stanley scorns—the glance !
The brilliant chief, irregularly great,
Frank, haughty, rash,— the Rupert of debate.

.   .   .   .   .

Yet who not listens with delightful smile,
To the pure Saxon of that silver style :
In the clear style a heart as clear is seen,
Prompt to the rash—revolting from the mean."

Sir Archibald Alison also bears the following testimony to his fame :—" He is, beyond all doubt, and by
" the admission of all parties, the most perfect orator of
" his day. His style of speaking differs essentially from
" that of the great statesmen of his own or the preceding
" age. His leading feature is neither the vehement de-

"clamation of Fox, nor the lucid narrative of Pitt, nor
"the classical fancy of Canning, nor the varied energy
"of Brougham. Capable, when he chooses, of rivalling
"any of these, illustrious in the line in which they
"excelled, the native bent of his mind leads him
"rather to a combination of their varied excellencies,
"but which combine, in a surprising manner, to form
"a graceful and attractive whole. At once playful
"and serious, eloquent and instructive, amusing and
"pathetic, his thoughts seem to flow from his
"lips in an unpremeditated stream, which at once
"delights and fascinates his hearers. None was ever
"tired while his speech lasted; no one ever saw him
"come to a conclusion without regret. He is capable
"at times of rising to the highest flights of oratory,
"is always thoroughly master of the subject on which
"he speaks, and never fails to place his views in the
"clearest and most favourable light." And the *Times*,
in speaking of the late Lord Aberdeen, says:—"Not
"only had Lord Aberdeen seen Fox and Pitt stand as
"Byron has described them—the two mountains,
"'Athos and Ida, with a dashing sea of eloquence
"'between'—he had listened with awe to the rolling
"thunders of Burke, he had witnessed the brilliant
"but harmless thunders of Sheridan, he had heard
"Granville and Grey in their prime. Whitebread and
"Wyndham he had heard volleying forth their cla-
"mours by the hour; and with all the inclination of

"an old man to depreciate the present and to laud the
"past, he has declared of these giants, of whom it is
"supposed that we are never more to see the like,
"that not one of them, as a speaker, is to be com-
"pared with our own Lord Derby, when Lord Derby
"is at his best."

At the present moment, when the Earl of Derby,
although advanced in life, is still in the zenith of his
political fame, it may be well to introduce here a
graphic sketch of his lordship's political position
upwards of twenty years since, as laid down at the
commencement of a merciless attack upon his lordship, in the December number for 1844, of the
Westminster Review. It is the spontaneous testimony of a bitter political enemy to the power and
influence of a rising statesman of the time :—

"Few public men of our time," says the writer,
"prime ministers scarcely excepted, have been
"charged with weightier responsibilities, or actively
"engaged in a greater number and variety of political
"affairs of first class importance than Lord Stanley.
"He has held, successively. two of our most impor-
"tant state secretaryships, in each instance, during a
"critical period, with questions of the utmost urgency
"and magnitude pressing for a prompt solution; in
"each instance, with an overpowering parliamentary
"majority at his command, ready to register in the
"statute book his individual convictions of the right

"and expedient. He has been charged with the
"reform of the greatest abuse known to the British
"empire—the Protestant Church of Ireland; with
"the regeneration of the parliamentary constitution
"of Ireland; with the suppression of Irish disturb-
"ances, and the extinguishment of Irish discontents.
"It has been his fortune to be ruler of the British
"Colonies, first, at a time, when, in our West India
"Islands, the whole framework of society had to be
"taken to pieces, and re-constructed: and, when in
"Canada, the accumulated grievances of a quarter of
"a century were calling for instant redress, with
"rebellion and civil war as the alternative; and
"again, at a period, when, in the newest of our set-
"tlements, the most hopeful and promising experi-
"ment in colonization that modern times have seen,
"had to be aided and guided towards a successful
"result. He has twice held office in strong govern-
"ments, and once been an influential leader of
"opposition against a weak one. Even his neutrality
"and inaction have been powerfully felt in the world
"of politics. He has not only led parties—he has
"held the balance between parties. Seldom has a
"public man possessed a larger share of real parlia-
"mentary power than that wielded by Lord Stanley,
"in the early part of the session of 1835, at the head
"of some half dozen waverers, when a ministry and an
"opposition—each numbering their three hundred

"and more—waited to learn their fate from his lips.
"All things taken together, we may say that few
"statesmen have had larger powers and weightier
"duties, both in and out of office, than Lord Stanley."

Such is the recorded influence which his lordship
is said to have possessed, as Lord Stanley, more than
twenty years since. May we not exclaim, how infi-
nitely greater is the moral and political influence
of the Earl of Derby at the present moment! But it
is not by the course which he has taken in the world
of politics alone, that his lordship has commended
himself to the affectionate respect and admiration of
his countrymen. Although having been absorbed,
during a life time, in the cares and anxieties of political strife and contention, he has nevertheless availed
himself of some stolen leisure hours for the exercise
of those literary and classical abilities, which, in so
eminent a degree, he possesses. It is true that he
has not contributed very much to our stock of literature, and, when we consider how constantly and
uniformly each succeeding year of his life has been
closely devoted to the service of the state, our only
feeling of surprise is that he has found time and
opportunity to contribute anything at all. If, however, he had never given the world any other proof
of his high classical and literary attainments, his able
translation of Homer is sufficient to convince every one
of his elevated intellectual powers. But we have also,

other literary compositions from his pen, amongst
them, one of an interesting character, as bearing upon
his religious feelings and views.   In the year 1849,
he published a work, entitled "Conversations on the
Parables of the New Testament," which reveals deep
thought, and a profound knowledge and appreciation
of Biblical literature.   His splendid and eloquent
address at Glasgow, on his installation as Lord Rector
of the University, at the close of the year 1834, as
well as that at Oxford, when installed as Chancellor
of the University, in the year 1853, both testify to
his high intellectual attainments.   It is not, however, to the field of politics, or of literature alone,
that we must look for those benefits which his lordship has conferred on his country, or the moral and
intellectual advancement of society which he has
promoted.   Beyond these his lordship has given
abundant proof of a profound regard for the material
well-being of his fellow creatures.   It is not our intention to dwell upon the subject, for it is one of too
delicate a nature, but there is one occasion to which
we must allude, as exemplifying, in an eminent
degree, his lordship's sympathy with human suffering.
We all too well remember the deep privations which
had to be endured in the manufacturing districts,
during the continuance of the civil war in America.
The occasion demanded, and evoked, the most un-
bounded charity on the part of the wealthy, and the

princely liberality of the Earl of Derby in that trying
emergency reflected greater honour on his lordship
than any coronet could confer. The writer well re-
members being present at the public county meeting
which was held at Manchester, on the 2nd of December, 1862, for the purpose of raising a fund for
relieving the sufferers. On that occasion, the noble
Earl not only contributed a munificent sum for the
amelioration of their condition, (£5000) but his great
talents were also there dedicated to the furtherance
of as noble an object as any in support of which they
had ever before been employed. He spoke on the
occasion with a depth of feeling amounting to religious fervour, and never were his lordship's transcen-
dant oratorical powers and eloquence more usefully
exercised than in connexion with a gathering which
had for its object the assistance of a community
reduced to the last state of physical suffering and
starvation, by an intestine war which will ever be
memorable in the annals of history.

His exordium on the occasion was marked by a
depth of feeling which showed his profound sympathy
for the sufferers on whose behalf the meeting had
been convened. "We are met together," said his
lordship, "upon an occasion which must call forth
"the most painful, and which at the same time ought
"to excite—and I am sure will excite—the most
"kindly feelings of our human nature. We are met

"to consider the best means of palliating—would to
"God I could say removing—a great national cala-
"mity, the like whereof, in modern times, has never
"been witnessed in this favoured land; a calamity
"which it was impossible for those who are the
"greatest sufferers to foresee, or, if they had foreseen,
"to take any step to avoid; a calamity which, though
"shared by the nation at large, falls more particularly,
"and with the heaviest weight, upon this hitherto
"prosperous and wealthy district; a calamity which
"has converted this teeming hive of industry into a
"stagnant desert, comparatively of inactivity and
"idleness, and converted that which has been the
"source of our greatest wealth into the deepest abyss
"of impoverishment; a calamity which has im-
"poverished the wealthy, which has brought distress
"upon those who have been somewhat above the
"world, by the exercise of frugal industry; and a
"calamity which has reduced honest and struggling
"poverty to a state of absolute and humiliating desti-
"tution.   It is to meet this calamity that we are met
"together, and to add our means and our assistance
"to those efforts which have been so nobly made
"throughout the country generally."   His lordship
then proceeded to point out the great amount of distress and destitution which prevailed, by showing the
enormous increase in the numbers of those who were
receiving parochial relief in the manufacturing dis-

tricts of Lancashire, in addition to those who were
relieved by the several local committees in the various
towns throughout the county; and having further
shown the very large excess in the amount of deposits
withdrawn from the savings' banks, the noble Earl
observed :—"We may figure to ourselves the amount
"of difficulty, sorrow, and privation, which that
"amount represents. It represents the blighted hopes
"for life of many a family; it represents the small
"sums set aside by honest, frugal, persevering in-
"dustry, by years of toil and self-dependence, in the
"hope of it being, as it has been in many cases before,
"the foundations of colossal fortunes; it represents
"the hopes for his family of many an industrious
"artisan; and it is the first step in that downward
"progress which leads him to destitution and to
"pauperism. The first step is the withdrawal of the
"savings of honest industry from the savings' banks;
"then comes the sacrifice of some little cherished
"article of furniture, the cutting off of some little
"indulgence, the sacrifice of that which makes in his
"home an additional appearance of comfort and
"happiness; the sacrifice, one by one, of articles of
"furniture, until at last the well-conducted, honest,
"frugal, saving artisan finds himself on a level with
"the idle, the dissipated, and the impoverished—
"obliged to pawn the very clothes of his family, and
"only prevented by a noble independence from be-

"coming dependent upon public or private charity,
"in the emphatic words of the dialect of his county,
"declaring, 'Nay, but we would 'clem' first.'" After
reading the resolution which he had to propose, the
effect of which was that the patient submission with
which the working classes in the manufacturing
districts had borne their sufferings and privations
entitled them to the warmest sympathies of their
fellow-countrymen, his lordship said:—"I cannot lose
"the opportunity of asking this great assembly, with
"what feelings this state of things should be con-
"templated by those in higher circumstances. In
"the first place, I will say with all reverence, that it
"is a subject for deep national humiliation. We have
"been accustomed for years to look with pride upon
"the enormous wealth of the manufacturing portion
"of the industry of this country; we have seen,
"within the last twelve or fourteen years, the con-
"sumption of cotton in Europe extending from 50,000
"to 90,000 bales per week; we have seen the weight
"of cotton exported from this country amounting to
"no less than 983,000,000 lbs. in a single year; and
"we have been accustomed to look down upon those
"less fortunate districts where wealth and fortune are
"built upon a less secure foundation, to consider the
"cotton manufactures as a security against the possi-
"bility of war between us and the cotton producing
"districts, and to hold that in the cotton manufacture

" lies the great strength of the country, and of future
" national prosperity and peace.   I am afraid we have
" looked at this too much in the spirit of the Assyrian
" monarch of old, to whom the words were called
" forth, 'Thy kingdom is departed from thee.'   That
" which was his pride became his humiliation, and
" that which has been our pride has become our
" humiliation and punishment.   That which we have
" considered the source of our wealth, and the sure
" foundation upon which we have built, has been itself
" the cause of our humiliation.   The reed upon which
" we have leaned has gone through the hand that
" pressed upon it, and has pierced us to the heart."

Whether, then, we regard the Earl of Derby as a
statesman, a scholar, or a philanthropist, he is equally
entitled to our admiration and esteem; and in his
person the illustrious House of Stanley maintains its
ancient, loyal, and honourable traditions.

CHAPTER IX.

THE RIGHT HON. LORD STANLEY, M.P., SECRETARY OF STATE FOR FOREIGN AFFAIRS.

THE Right Hon. Lord Stanley, now Chief Secretary for Foreign Affairs in his father's administration, is undoubtedly the most rising, and, at the same time, the most popular statesman of the day. It would almost appear that the genius and administrative ability of the Stanleys are now becoming intuitive, for although, from physical causes, Lord Stanley is not his father's equal in oratory, we very much question whether he is not, comparatively young as he is, a more profound thinker, whilst so far as regards aptitude for public business and real hard work, we venture to say that he has not an equal in the House. Lord Stanley is in every sense a remarkable man. Study and devotion to public life seems to be the object of his existence, and although surrounded by all the aids and appliances for the indulgence of luxurious ease and enjoyment, he appears to be indifferent to them all, preferring, perhaps for "the love of it," a life of what may be called absolute drudgery in

the service of the public. He is the type of a class
peculiarly his own, if we may be permitted to make
use of the somewhat anomalous expression. He is the
most self-denying public man who has appeared before
the world during the present generation, and we are
bold enough to say that there is not a statesman in
England who has so many friends, and as few enemies, for the former consist of all parties in the
state and the country, whilst the latter are scarcely to
be found amongst any class of society, even with
the aid of the most powerful microscope. Lord
Stanley is a philosopher, in the true sense of the
term, and what follows will prove it.

Edward Henry, Lord Stanley, was born at
Knowsley, on the 21st of July, 1826, about a week
after his father, the present Earl of Derby, was
elected a member of Parliament for the borough of
Preston, when opposed by William Cobbett, as one
of three other candidates. He obtained the early
portion of his education at Rugby, and from thence
he proceeded to Trinity College, Cambridge, where
he graduated, until the year 1848. During his stay
at Cambridge, that intense study commenced for
which he has since been so pre-eminently distinguished in more matured life. When he quitted his
college, in the year 1848, he was in the first class in
classics, in addition to which, he took high honours
in the mathematical tripos, gaining a medal for decla-

mation, besides a number of other prizes. Before leaving college he took the degree of Master of Arts.

The year before completing his studies, 1847, he attained his majority, the event being celebrated in the autumn of that year at Knowsley, by a series of festivities, which extended over an entire week. The invitations included not only the nobility and gentry of the county, but were also liberally supplied to the tradesmen and all classes in Liverpool and the surrounding towns in Lancashire; in addition to which the park and grounds at Knowsley were thrown open to the general public, who were invited to partake of the liberal hospitalities of the Earl. Nor were the tenantry and labourers on the estates forgotten. Immense marquees had been erected in several parts of the desmesne, in which every one in any way connected with the estates was cordially welcomed and regaled; and throughout the whole of the week Knowsley was one continued scene of gaeity and rejoicing. It was on this occasion that Lord Stanley, or rather the Hon. Mr. Stanley (for his grandfather, the late Earl, was then alive) first publicly gave evidence of his talents and abilities. A grand banquet was given in honour of the occasion in a spacious and elegantly decorated marquee, immediately adjacent to the hall. The scene presented was about as gorgeous a sight of its kind as the writer, who was present, ever witnessed. The walls

of the spacious apartment itself were covered with
immense mirrors from the floor to the ceiling, which,
with the surrounding decorations, contributed to im-
part additional effect to the brilliancy produced by
the presence of an immense assemblage of the aristocracy and the *elite* of the country. The late Earl,
together with the present Earl and Countess, and
the whole of the Knowsley family and their friends,
were of course present, and we should here add, that
a spacious gallery or balcony had been provided for
the ladies, which materially added to the general
effect. When the young patrician and heir to the
Earldom, fresh from his collegiate studies, rose to
address the company assembled, the greatest possible
interest was of course manifested to hear his maiden
speech. At the outset there was naturally a little
trepidation, but a few minutes sufficed to show his
intellectual and oratorical abilities, and there was no
difficulty in predicting for him that brilliant future
which has already in his early life been realized.

In the early part of the year 1848, Lord Stanley came
forward as a candidate for Lancaster, but was defeated,
and in a few months afterwards he left England for
the purpose of making himself acquainted with our
West Indian and North American Colonies. After
having travelled through the West Indies he visited
Canada, and subsequently went over a considerable
portion of the United States. Whilst he was travelling

in America, in December 1848, he unexpectedly received the information that he had been elected member for King's Lynn, in place of the late Lord George Bentinck. On his return home from his travels in the West Indies and America, he very soon proved to the world that he had not been idle during his absence, for in a very short time after his arrival in England, he published a pamphlet entitled "Claims and Resources of the West Indian Colonies." This interesting publication, which was addressed in the form of a letter to the Right Hon. W. E. Gladstone, showed close observation. It recommended the repeal of the export duties as a boon to the planters. In the session of 1850 he took his seat in the House of Commons, and it was shortly after the publication of the above named pamphlet that he made his maiden speech in the House, his subject being the state of our West Indian Colonies in reference to the Sugar question. The speech was admitted by both sides of the House to be a perfect success, and both Lord Palmerston and Mr. Gladstone warmly complimented his lordship on the occasion. It may safely be stated that from that day Lord Stanley's parliamentary status was secured. The speech was the subject of considerable conversation in the precincts of the House at the time it was made, on grounds appertaining to something beyond its own intrinsic merits. About the same period the present

Sir Robert Peel—his father being then alive—was placed in a similar position in the House to the noble lord, and whilst it was considered by many that the son of the great commoner, from whom much was expected, had disappointed the hopes of his friends, the descendant of the Earl of Derby had made "a decided hit," and put the son of the baronet into the shade. It is not too much to say that subsequent events have verified these opinions. In the year 1851 Lord Stanley followed up his first pamphlet with another on the same subject, also addressed to Mr. Gladstone, entitled "Further Facts connected with "the West Indies." In this publication he enforced the views put forward in his first pamphlet, together with several remarks on the general condition of the Colonies. Travel, and a determination to see and judge for himself as to the condition and resources of our foreign dependencies, appear strongly to have animated his lordship, and accordingly we now find him again leaving England in 1851 for the far distant regions of India. He travelled as far eastward as Hindostan, exploring the district included in the Bengal presidency, when in April 1852, by a singular coincidence—in America he learnt of his election for King's Lynn—he received the intelligence that he had been appointed Under-Secretary of State in the Foreign Office, in the ministry just formed by his father. Having received this information, he returned

home, his researches being thus abruptly ended.
On his arrival in England he at once took his seat in
the House, and entered upon the duties of office, but
the first ministry of Lord Derby having a short
existence, he soon found himself in the ranks of the
Opposition.   Although his travels in India and his
intended researches in that country had been
interfered with by the recal home to which we have
already referred, he took advantage in the House of
what he had experienced there, notwithstanding that
he was now on the Opposition side, and in the session
of 1853 he brought forward a resolution, the principle
of which involved extensive reforms in the management of our Indian territory, but it was not carried.
The spirit of this resolution was however subsequently
carried out under Lord Derby's government of 1858,
when Lord Stanley was at the India Board.   The
Church-rate question, which has frequently been
under the consideration of the House, but which it
has hitherto been unable to settle, came under
discussion during the session of 1853, when his lordship spoke strongly in favour of its unconditional
repeal, thus, on this subject differing from the great
majority of his own party, but it is well understood
that—especially on all subjects in which what he
considers undue religious imposts are involved—his
Conservatism is of an exceedingly liberal character.
On every subsequent occasion when this subject has

been brought before the House he has uniformly voted for the abolition of the rate.

We pass over the general proceedings in Parliament from 1853 to 1858, during which his lordship continued to sit on the Opposition benches. When the Earl of Derby's second ministry was formed, in 1858, Lord Stanley was in the first instance appointed to the office of Colonial Secretary, but on the resignation of the Earl of Ellenborough he succeeded him as President of the Board of Control, and it was whilst he was in that position that he availed himself of the opportunity of bringing in the India Bill, which he carried through Parliament, and which had the effect of sweeping away what was unfavorably known as the double government, and substituting in its stead the India Board, with a Secretary of State for India at its head, the last named official taking equal rank with the four other great Secretaries of State. Under the provisions of the India Bill the President of the Board of Control was abolished, and Lord Stanley himself became the first Secretary of State for India under the new arrangement, having been sworn in before her Majesty on the 2nd of September, 1858. We may here observe, in proof of Lord Stanley being a general favourite beyond the immediate circle of his own political party, that in the year 1855, on the death of Sir William Molesworth, who held the office of

Colonial Secretary under Lord Palmerston, the noble viscount placed the vacant office at the disposal of Lord Stanley, which, however, his lordship declined to accept. It may be safely affirmed that the parliamentary career of Lord Stanley, so far, has been one unclouded success, in every department of the Government which has been entrusted to his charge. We question whether he has ever been accused of either a blunder or a mistake, and, indeed, it is scarcely to be supposed that one so calm and thoughtful, who never takes action on any one given subject until he has thoroughly and deliberately examined it in all its bearings, should be led into error or compromise his position. During the short time he was at the Colonial Office, in 1858, his management of that department was never called in question; his subsequent conduct at his newly constituted India Board, including the part he took in the re-organisation of the management of our Indian possessions, met with unqualified approval ; whilst to crown all his previous efforts, the admirable manner in which he is at the present moment conducting our foreign relations under circumstances of more than ordinary difficulty —the ability, the tact, and the discretion which he manifests in every step which he takes, commands the universal approval and esteem of both Parliament and the country, and we sincerely believe that no minister ever held the reins of power in whom the nation at large had such implicit confidence. But Lord Stanley is not only a statesman. He is something more. We have said that his is a life of study and almost drudgery in the service of the public. In some form or other he is always working for them. He cannot afford to be idle. If he is not actually engaged in the senate, or writing dispatches in the bureau of the department with which he is connected, he is closely occupied in some kind of employment for promoting the social and political advancement of his fellows, and thus we find that some years ago he wrote a pamphlet, which, however, was only printed for private circulation, recommending that the parliamentary blue books should be epitomised and printed at the Government cost, and supplied to all mechanics' institutes, as well as to the metropolitan and provincial press, for the purpose of furnishing the public, on every subject coming before the legislature, with the same accurate and authoritative information which is now supplied to the members. In a word, Lord Stanley, whether we regard him in a political or a social aspect, is one of the very foremost men of the age, and the splendid future which lies before him is one that few of his contemporaries can hope for.

CHAPTER X.

THE present narrative would not be complete without some description of the noble and extensive domain of Knowsley, which has been in possession of the illustrious family forming the subject of the foregoing pages, for a period now bordering upon nearly five hundred years. The Knowsley property was in the possession of the Lathom family previous to its passing to the Stanleys. In the fourteenth century Sir Robert de Lathom married Catherine, daughter and heiress of Sir Thomas de Knowsley, and thus by this marriage Knowsley became the property of the Lathoms. At a later period, as has already been stated in the preceding pages, Sir John Stanley, the founder of the House of Derby, married Isabel, the daughter and heiress of Sir Thomas Lathom, of Lathom and Knowsley, grandson of the above named Sir Robert de Lathom, and it was by this marriage that the celebrated domain of Knowsley, which now possesses a more than usual historical interest, passed to the Stanley family, and with the exception of the period of the Civil War and the Commonwealth, has ever since remained in their possession.

At the time when Knowsley was first owned by the Stanleys, consequent upon the alliance just referred to, Lathom House continued the principal residence of the family, and it was not until after the memorable siege of Lathom House, during the time of James the seventh Earl, when his Countess played such a heroic part, that the Stanleys took up their abode at Knowsley as their principal mansion. In earlier times, before the matrimonial alliance which transferred it to the Stanleys, Knowsley is said to have been little more than a hunting seat for the sport and enjoyment of the Lathom family, and its character in this respect seems to have been maintained until the year 1485, when Henry the Seventh visited his mother, the Countess of Thomas, the first Earl of Derby, in a few months after the great battle of Bosworth Field.

There is no park in Lancashire, nor indeed in the northern counties of England, with the exception of that of the Earl of Lonsdale in Westmoreland, which can at all compare either in extent or picturesque beauty, with that of Knowsley. It is situated on high ground, and on all sides the view is extensive and commanding. It is between fourteen and fifteen miles in circumference, and occupies an area

of about 2500 acres, or upwards of 12,000,000 square
yards. It is surrounded throughout by exceedingly
handsome and ornamental walls, there being at
intervals no less than eleven lodges and entrances by
which communication with the mansion to the
different towns and districts in the surrounding
neighbourhood is afforded. All the lodges, with the
exception of the Liverpool entrance, have massive
and handsome wrought iron gates. The entrance to
the park and mansion from the Liverpool lodge is the
most commanding of the whole, and is regarded as
the main or principal approach to the domain. The
lodge itself is a large and imposing stone edifice. In
the centre is a noble arch, supported by a round
tower on the right, and a square tower on the left, the
arch being surmounted by the Derby arms, with the
family motto inscribed. Large oak doors for the
carriage entrance, are placed under the central arch,
and there is also a door at the side entrance under
the square tower, over which is the following
inscription:—" Bring good news, and knock boldly."

The scenery in the park, which is beautifully un-
dulating, is exceedingly varied, abounding in charming
lawn and woodland views, with noble groups of trees
in different elevated positions. From almost every
part of the park, but more especially that portion of
it more immediately in front of the hall, the view of
the surrounding country is commanding and beau-

tiful, not being confined to inland scenery, but
embracing on the west, a splendid marine and sea
prospect. The course of the Mersey, with its opening
to the Irish Sea, and the beautiful and romantic
Welsh mountain scenery appears in the distance,
opening up to the spectator a charming and picturesque
view. The park throughout is magnificently wooded,
more especially that portion which is known as the
Gladewoods, in which there is one large tree constantly
attracting much attention and interest, from the fact
of its having been twisted in the stem, either by some
freak of nature, or other singular agency, which gives
it the appearance of a huge cork-screw. The park
also contains a large and artistically arranged lake,
upwards of ninety acres in extent. This fine sheet
of water is called the " Large Lake," or the " White
Man's Dam," the latter name having been given to it
in consequence of the embankment giving way during
a storm, about seventy-five years since, when the lake,
which is situated on a high level, rushed down into
the lower portions of the park, destroying trees and
everything it its progress, including the Mizzy and
China temple lakes in the pleasure grounds, and even
threatening to inundate the mansion. Near the head
of the lake there is a nude statue, called the " White
Man," the tradition being that the statue was found
in the lake. On the west side of the lake is a fine
boat-house, constructed of stone, tastefully filled with

antique furniture, and varied specimens of natural history. Near this large lake is the "Mizzy Dam" or lake, to which allusion has just been made ; and near the south front of the hall there is another fine lake, beyond the hall and pleasure grounds, called the "China Temple Dam;" both these two last named lakes receiving their water from the Large Lake or White Man's Dam. A large portion of the eastern side of the park, consisting of several hundreds of acres, forms the "Deer Park," in which there are numerous herds of the red, fallow, and other deer. The gardens and pleasure grounds, which are very extensive, are most artistically laid out, and beautifully decorated with works of art.

The mansion at Knowsley has been on several occasions enlarged, and to a great extent re-built. On the occasion of Henry the Seventh coming to Knowsley, on a visit to his mother, the Countess of Thomas, first Earl of Derby, as already named, the Earl considerably enlarged the mansion for the King's reception, erecting a spacious stone building, with two round towers at the south front, but which now have the square tower—inside of which is the banquetting hall—and the colonnade front on the east, and the steward's offices on the west, the latter being connected with the mansion by a stone archway. The royal apartments were contained between the two round towers, and are still called "the King's Chambers."

In the year 1552, Edward, third Earl of Derby, exchanged his house in London, called Derby Place, for considerable lands adjoining Knowsley, and this exchange largely increased the Knowsley estates. In subsequent years the Earl made still further additions to the mansion. Little if any alterations or additions appear to have been made from that period to the time of James, the tenth Earl, who, it may be said, almost re-built the mansion, which, to a great extent had been suffered to fall into decay from the period of the Civil War, in the time of James, the seventh Earl. The principal part of the mansion, as it now stands, may, indeed, be said to have been built by the tenth Earl. A portion of the building, namely, the west or carriage approach front, is constructed of red brick, the quoins and designs to the long range of windows, being of stone. Although this includes some of the most ancient portions of the building, the arrangement imparts to it a comparatively modern aspect. This front, which is the most extensive portion of the edifice, is divided into three equal parts, of uniform height, the main entrance being in the centre, which is approached by a double flight of steps to the principal floor; the whole being surmounted by a balustrade, with chaste and artistic scroll ornaments. The palatial and magnificent drawing rooms, as also the choice and splendid picture gallery, are also included in this portion of the edifice. The east front of the mansion is uniform in architectural style and finish with the west elevation, being like the latter, built of red brick, with stone dressings to the windows. The private chapel attached to the hall is on this side of the building, the exterior being marked by a projecting wing. A few years ago, this chapel, which is tolerably spacious, was renovated and re-fitted throughout, and is now a very convenient, as well as an ornamental ecclesiastical interior. In the re-arrangement of the chapel, the Gothic style has been adopted, the whole of the timber work, including the seats, being Dantzic oak. The pulpit, which is placed at the east end of the chapel, in unison with long prevailing custom, is of tasteful and appropriate design, and richly and elaborately carved. The panels on the sides of the seats are also artistically carved, and on each side of the pulpit there are two massive oak chairs, beautifully carved, the pulpit, seats, and chairs, chastely harmonising with each other. The south facade of the edifice, which is, to a great extent, built of red sandstone, has more claim to architectural beauty and effect than those which have already been described. It is castellated in style, and contains three divisions, namely, the colonnade front, the large square tower forming the banquetting hall, and the erection known as the King's apartments, including the two round towers, built as has already been stated, by Thomas, the first Earl of Derby, on the

occasion of the visit to Knowsley of Henry the
Seventh, in 1495. It has been observed that that
portion of the hall erected specially to receive King
Henry, was originally entirely distinct from the rest
of the mansion, but was at a subsequent period
connected with the rest of the pile. Even in those
comparatively early days masonry and handicraft
must have arrived at a considerable state towards
perfection, for although this portion of the hall forms
one of its most prominent parts, and consists of a
drawing-room, dining-room, staircase, bed-chamber,
dressing-room, page's-room, a bed-chamber for the
Lord-Chamberlain, and a dining-room for the members
of the King's household, it was commenced and
completed within the period of a few months. Edward,
the twelfth Earl of Derby, erected the red stone portion
of this, the principal frontage of the mansion, in
order to give a reception befitting royalty, to George
the-Fourth, who at that time was Prince Regent. The
erection of this part of the building occupied a considerable period, commencing in the early part of the
year 1820, and the large square tower, which forms
the banquetting hall, was not completed until 1821.
That portion of the south front erected by Edward,
the twelfth Earl, which is the most prominent, is the
colonnade part of it. All the colonnades, which are of
stone, and painted, are one above the other. Six pair
of columns, of the Doric order of architecture, support .

the base colonnade, and the open spaces between these columns admit of the gravel walk in front being approached by a descent of two steps from the floor of the colonnade. The style of architecture of the upper colonnade columns differs from those supporting the base, although they are the same in number. They are of the Ionic order, having between each two of the columns an artistic and ornamental railing. Opposite the pillars, within the two colonnades, are crescent-formed recesses, fitted with seats, and over the entrance to the upper colonnade, which is from the interior, is a massive gilt panel fixed in the wall in front, representing in *basso-relievo*, the "Expulsion of Adam "and Eve from Paradise." Above the centre of the upper colonnade appear the arms of the family, and on the large stone tablet which supports it is the following inscription, which, although it has already been given in that portion of the volume (page 92) having reference to James, tenth Earl, it is necessary here to repeat :—
" James, Earl of Derby, Lord of Man and the Isles,
" Grandson of James, Earl of Derby, and of Charlotte,
"daughter of Claude, Duke de la Tremouile, whose
" husband, James, was beheaded at Bolton, XV. Oct.,
" MDCLII., for strenuously adhering to Charles the
" Second, who refused a Bill passed unanimously by
"both Houses of Parliament, for restoring to the
" family the estate, lost by his loyalty to him,
" MDCCXXXII." Considerable doubt has been

thrown on the historical accuracy of this inscription, and Baines, in his History of Lancashire, remarks upon it, "a Bill was passed in 16—17, Charles the "Second, by which he (Charles, the eighth Earl) was "restored to blood, from which it would appear that "the author of the inscription (James, the tenth Earl) "was not deeply versed in the history of his family." The north front of the mansion is also of red stone, and like the rest of the building, is two stories high. The upper story contains what are known as the "batchelors' apartments," and the lower story is appropriated to domestic purposes and servants' apartments.

The interior of the mansion possesses no less interesting and attractive features than its external architectural appearance. Within the last few years a grand staircase, thirty feet by twenty-seven feet, formed of most elaborately carved oak, has been erected opposite the west vestibule, which has materially added to the already noble appearance of the interior as we pass through the entrance hall. After proceeding along the entrance hall the visitor is ushered into two really magnificent drawing-rooms, most exquisitely and tastefully fitted *en suite*. The walls of these drawing-rooms are decorated and enriched by several fine historical and other paintings, including Rembrandt's celebrated picture of "Belshazzar's Feast," the admirable construction of the apartment in which it is exhibited admitting of this truly grand work of art being viewed to the greatest advantage. In addition to this fine painting there are also several other choice pictures by the old masters, in other parts of the two drawing rooms. Adjoining the drawings is that portion of the interior known as the stucco gallery, in which the connoisseur in art may spend hours of profit and pleasure. The walls of the gallery are covered with choice gems from the pencils of Rubens, Teniers, and other celebrated artists. At the end of the stucco gallery is the apartment known as the "mahogany chamber," being thus named in consequence of the whole of the fittings, wainscotting, with the furniture to correspond, being of mahogany. Leaving the stucco gallery, and the mahogany chamber, the stucco room is entered. This apartment is so called from its being exclusively adorned with specimens of stucco-work, including beautiful medallion heads of the twelve Cæsars, in *basso relievo*. It may here be stated that this was one of the apartments erected by James, the tenth Earl, when he, to a great extent, rebuilt Knowsley. It was, in his day, used as one of the ball-rooms for the visitors entertained there, but it is now classed amongst the drawing-rooms. Immediately adjacent to the stucco-room are "the King's chambers." An interesting feature in these apartments is the fact that in one of the rooms is the bedstead used by the

14

Prince Regent, when he visited Knowsley, in 1821, and the royal visit is commemorated by a large Prince of Wales' feathers, in gold and crimson velvet, being exhibited on the top of the footboard. One of the most interesting historical portraits connected with the Derby family is exhibited on the walls of this apartment. It is that of Charlotte de la Tremouile, Countess of James, the seventh Earl, and the heroic defender of Lathom House, during the siege. The picture represents the Countess when she is receiving the last insolent message of Rigby, calling upon her to surrender, and when after reading the letter she tears it up, and exclaims "Trumpet, tell "that insolent rebel, Rigby, that if he presumes to "send another message within this place, 1 will have "the messenger hanged up at the gates." Besides this valuable work of art, so highly prized by the family, by reason of the historical reminiscences which it awakens, there are also several other choice paintings in this apartment. The rooms immediately adjoining are all designated "the King's apartments," and consist of dressing-room, sitting, and other rooms, one of which, the walls being covered with miniature paintings, is called the "miniature room." It will thus be seen that the several apartments which have already been named are each and all invested with peculiar features of attractiveness, but perhaps the most magnificent apartment in the mansion is the splendid banquetting room within the massive square tower, which, as has already been stated, was built by Edward, the twelfth Earl. This truly gorgeous interior is entered by a massive carved oak door, sixteen feet in height. The hall is large and spacious, and fifty feet in height. It is throughout fitted up in gothic style, including the ceiling, which is pierced in the centre, by means of which light is admitted by a lantern light, and suspended from the ceiling is a massive and elegant chandelier. The furniture throughout the hall is of elaborately carved oak, thus harmonizing with the gothic fittings of the noble apartment. Prominent amongst the furniture is an immense carved oak sideboard, which is said to have been in the family for several centuries, and is of great antiquity. The carving is exquisitely rich and artistic. In addition to this choice and rare article of banquetting requirements there are also two other sideboards at the north end of the hall. On the east and west sides of the hall, respectively, there are two large fire places, with massive white marble mantels. The drapery and general furniture is elegant whilst chaste, and the artistic decorations superb. In this grand apartment the visitor may look for hours with admiration, on the portraits of the Earls and Countesses of Derby of past ages, for here they are all exhibited from the earliest times. Two of the most striking and prominent are the portraits of Thomas, the first Earl of Derby, and his Countess, mother to Henry the Seventh, who was married to the Earl under the peculiar conditions already referred to. As stated by the author before, quoted (see page 21-2) the Countess's portrait represents her " with uplifted hands, in the attitude " of prayer—her breviary laid open on the cushion " before her. She is arrayed in the muffled habit of a " religionist, and looks the incarnation of a saint " already half exhaled." The portraits of James the seventh Earl and his Countess, are also peculiarly attractive amongst the family collection. The miscellaneous paintings in this apartment are too numerous to particularize. They include many of the finest productions of art in existence, amongst them being "the Passage of the Red Sea," the " Entry " into the Land of Promise," " Moses with Aaron and " Hur on Mount Horeb, interceding with God on " behalf of the Israelites, who are fighting with the " Amalekites, at Rephidim," and " Joshua commanding " the Sun." There is also amongst the number, a portrait of Archdeacon Rutter, Chaplain to James the seventh Earl, whom he attended to the scaffold. This painting is said to have been found at Knowsley only a few years ago. In addition to the above there is a further portrait of Charlotte de la Tremouile in her weeds, after the execution of her husband. The picture gallery itself, which is ninety feet in length, by eleven feet in width, also contains a very numerous and valuable collection, by most of the old masters, amongst others, including Vandyke, Salvator Rosa, Rubens, Vanderwent, Guido, Claude Loraine, Correggio, Teniers, Poussin, &c., &c. " Christ delivering the " keys to St. Peter," " Seneca in the bath," " Head of " John the Baptist," " Christ and the Woman of " Samaria," and " the Expulsion from Eden," are included in the collection. The great portion of the paintings by the old masters, which form such a prominent feature in this almost unequalled collection, were purchased and brought to Knowsley, by James the tenth Earl. There are two very ancient pieces of furniture at the hall. They consist of two carved oak cupboards, one of which is dated 1501, and has several scriptural pieces carved on the panels. The date shows that it has probably been in possession of the family even so early as the time of the first Earl, who died in 1504. There is also another carved oak side board, the carving having been executed by the Countess of Charles, the eighth Earl, inasmuch as it bears her name, " Helena Countess of Derby." The library is rich in literary lore, and well worth the close inspection of the visitor to this princely mansion. In addition to the valuable volumes which it contains, there is also a collection of family portraits, in cases, with a short biographical notice in each. The library also contains the chair in which James, the seventh

Earl sat when he was beheaded at Bolton. This
chair, although to all appearance ebony, being
apparently black, is nevertheless composed of oak. It
has a low carved back, with spiral spindles. A few
years ago it was presented to the present Earl of
Derby, by James Hardcastle, Esq., of Bolton, that
family having had in it their possession for several
generations. On a brass plate on the chair is the
following inscription :—" This chair of the great Earl
" of Derby, at his martyrdom, was presented by James
" Hardcastle, of Bolton-le-Moors, to the Right Hon.
" Edward Geoffrey, Earl of Derby." The present
stables at Knowsley, which are said to be the most
extensive and complete of any in the country, were
built by the late Earl of Derby, at an estimated cost
of more than £30,000.

Perhaps more royal visits have been made to
Knowsley within the last few centuries, than to the
seat of any nobleman in England, and, as will be seen
from the foregoing sketch, there is no aristocratic
family in the country having greater facilities for
entertaining royal guests than are possessed by the
Earls of Derby. The "King's apartments," as they
are not inaptly termed, are specially set apart for
the reception of families connected with the monarchy
not only of our own, but also foreign countries, and
in years gone by they have frequently been applied
to this purpose, one of the more recent visits being

that of the Prince and Princess of Wales, with their suite, in the autumn of 1865.   On this occasion the Prince and Princess extended their stay to four days, one of which, October 31st, was set apart for a public visit to Liverpool.   The Prince and Princess, accompanied by the Earl and Countess of Derby, and a numerous party from Knowsley, in several carriages, arrived in Liverpool about eleven o'clock in the forenoon, and were most enthusiastically received.   The visit was made the occasion for a general holiday, and there was every outward demonstration of rejoicing.   All business was suspended for the day, which was kept as a complete holiday, in honour of the royal visit.   The several thoroughfares of the town were profusely decorated with flags, banners, and triumphal arches.   The shipping in the docks and river was similarly adorned, the forest of masts being covered with bunting, and the day being beautifully fine, with uninterrupted sunshine throughout, the scene presented was exceedingly animating.   The royal party, on arriving in Liverpool, were driven down to the Prince's pierhead, when they embarked on board a steamer, and made an excursion on the river, hundreds of small river steamers, gaily decorated, and crowded with spectators, accompanying them.   After disembarking, the Prince and Princess visited the Town Hall, St. George's Hall, and other public buildings, after which they returned to

Knowsley. In the year 1867, the Queen of the Netherlands paid a visit to Knowsley, remaining there as the guest of the noble Earl and Countess for a few days. The latest visit was that of the Prince and Princess Christian, Prince Arthur, and the Princess of Schleswig Holstein, in January, 1868. They arrived at Knowsley on Monday, the 6th of of January, and extended their visit to Saturday, the 11th, when they returned to London. On Wednesday, January 8th, Prince Christian and Prince Arthur went to Liverpool, and, accompanied by the Mayor, made an excursion on the river. On disembarking they drove to the Town Hall to luncheon, and afterwards visited the Free Library, where they were joined by the Princess Christian and the Princess of Schleswig Holstein. From the Free Library, the royal party proceeded to St. George's Hall, which was crowded with visitors. Here they were entertained to a performance on the great organ, the music having been selected by the Countess of Derby. On Thursday evening, January 9th, the royal party were entertained at a magnificent ball, by Edward Whitley, Esq., the Mayor. This entertainment was the most brilliant of its kind ever witnessed in Liverpool. Not only were the Town Hall rooms gorgeously decorated for the occasion, but the grand ball-room in that building was connected, by a temporary corridor, with the large exchange news-room, an apartment which is admitted to be one of the most magnificent in the world, whether as regards its architectural arrangements, or gorgeousness of decoration. The Princes and Princesses were accompanied to the ball by the Countess of Derby and a large party from Knowsley, and the entire number of guests present on the occasion was upwards of three thousand.

CHAPTER XI.

ARMS OF THE FAMILY.

THE arms and motto of the Stanley family are not without their interest, more especially as regards the crest of the eagle and child. The motto is *Sans Changer*—" Without changing." The arms contain three bucks' heads, cabossed, supported by a griffin and a buck; and the crest is an eagle preying on an infant in its cradle. It is popularly believed that this crest was first adopted by Sir Thomas Lathom, whose daughter, Isabel, was married to Sir John Stanley, the latter continuing the crest, which is maintained by the Stanley family to the present day. Other authorities state that the crest was not actually adopted until after the union of the Lathom and Stanley families by the marriage just named; but it is generally affirmed that its origin is due to the fact of a child having been found in an eagle's nest upon the estate, during the lifetime of Sir Thomas Lathom, who adopted and educated the child.

There are several fabulous traditions of the " Eagle and Child," gravely related, with all the circumstantiality of detail. It is recorded that Sir Thomas Lathom, who lived in the reign of Edward the Third, had no male issue; his only child, being Isabel, married to Sir John Stanley. Desirous, from early life, for a male heir to inherit his house and fortune, he had an intrigue with a young woman named Oskatel, the fruit of which was a son. The child was for some time altogether concealed from the Lathom family, Sir Thomas, although very anxious at once to adopt it, yet nevertheless being careful that its paternity should be kept secret. After a time, the following expedient was resorted to, for the purpose of the child being received into the family. Sir Thomas having entrusted the secret to an old and trustworthy servant on the estate, and taken counsel with him as to the best means by which the infant could be brought under the direct and immediate protection of the Lathom family, the latter suggested that as an eagle frequently formed her nest in a large thick wood in the most desolate part of the park, the child should be taken and laid there at the foot of the tree, as if brought there by the eagle, and that it should afterwards be accidentally discovered. Sir Thomas readily fell in with this proposition, and at once gave directions to the mother of the child to have the infant well fed and richly dressed early the next morning. At the same time, the domestic in Sir Thomas's confidence had instructions from the latter to call for the infant, and carry it to the foot of the tree which the eagle usually frequented, where it was to be laid and covered up, secured from all observation ; and the servant was to guard the child from all outward injury, either from beast or bird of prey ; and this was performed with all privacy.

Sir Thomas Lathom, now knowing that the child was laid at the foot of the tree, did not allow it to remain there long, but paid it an early visit, and immediately returned to the hall, and acquainted his lady and the family with the strange event. His lady and the household, accompanied by Sir Thomas, hastened to view such a miraculous discovery, and unanimously agreed that the infant's preservation in so dismal and dangerous a situation could be no less than a miracle ; and, upon finding it to be a male child, the good lady was enamoured with him, and concluded it to be the will of heaven that they should adopt him for their son and heir, which was eagerly agreed to by Sir Thomas.

The infant was thus carried home to the hall, and nursed and brought up, under the personal superintendence of the lady, with the same care and tenderness as if she had been his natural mother. He was baptised Oskatel de Lathom, but no one knew the reasons for his being called by that name, except his

mother, Mary Oskatel, and Sir Thomas. The child
was adopted by Sir Thomas and his lady, and educated as their heir; and was knighted by the King, at
Winchester, on the occasion of Sir John Stanley, his
presumed foster brother-in-law, overcoming the
French champion in single combat. Sir Thomas
Lathom, from that time, assumed for his crest an
eagle upon wing, turning her head back, and looking
in a sprightly manner as for something she had lost,
or was taken from her. Sir Thomas intended the
estates to descend to Sir Oskatel; but, in his old age,
and sometime before his death, his conscience smote
him, and, stating that his daughter, Isabel, Lady
Stanley, was his only legitimate offspring, and entitled
to his large possessions, he settled them upon that
lady and her heirs, for ever, publicly avowing that
Sir Oskatel was only his natural son. Sir Thomas
did not, however, leave poor Sir Oskatel, who had
now been deposed from his title and estates, without
being well provided for. He settled upon Sir Oskatel
and his heirs, for ever, the manors of Irlam and
Urmston, near Manchester, together with several
tracts of land in Lancashire and Cheshire, giving him
also the signet of his arms, with the crest assumed
by him for his sake. Sir Oskatel settled in the
County of Chester, and became the founder of the
family of Lathom, of Astbury.

There is a further tradition as to the origin of the

crest of the " Eagle and Child" in the Stanley family.
It is to the effect that Sir Thomas Lathom and his
Lady were one day taking their usual walk in the
park, and drawing near to that desert and wild situation where it was commonly reported an eagle built
her nest, they heard, on their approach, the cries of a
young child, which they ordered the servants attending to look for; who on search reported that it was in
the eagle's nest, which they directed to be taken
down. To their great surprise and wonder, it was
found on examination to contain a male infant dressed
in rich swaddling clothes, and they, having no male
issue, looked upon this child as a present sent from
heaven, and that it could be no less than the will of
God that they should immediately take him under
their care and protection, which they accordingly did,
and had him carefully nursed and baptised by the
name of Lathom. He became possessed of a large
estate, and at his death left an only daughter named
Isabel, whom Sir John Stanley married, who in
memory of this event took the " Eagle and Child" for
his crest, which has since been used by his noble
successors, the Earls of Derby.

Seacome altogether denies the correctness of this
story, as follows:—"Thus far goes the old tradition,
"which on examination and just information will
"appear to be mere fable and fiction, and highly
"improbable. Knowing the fury and violence with

" which an eagle strikes its prey, killing all it stoops
" to at one stroke, or before it leaves it, it must be
" allowed that it is morally impossible that a bird of
" prey, of the strength and rapacious nature which an
" eagle is known to possess should carry a live child to
" an airy height unhurt, which she never attends but
" when hatching or rearing her young, and then tears
" all to pieces she intends for herself or them as
" food, which they, while young, are unable to do
" for themselves."

Seacome is also doubtful whether the crest now
used by the Stanleys is the same as that adopted by
Sir Thomas Lathom, for he observes :—" Sir Oskatel
" being thus degraded and supplanted in the hopes
" and prospects of an immense fortune, was slighted
" and despised by his unthought-of rivals, who either
" to distinguish themselves, or in contempt and deri-
" sion of their spurious brother, took upon themselves
" the 'Eagle and Child' for their crest, in token of their
" conquest over him. This to me plainly manifests the
" variation of the two crests, and the reason of it. The
" eagle as represented in the Stanley's crest has actually
" made a prey of the child, whereas Sir Thomas Lathom's
" crest implies a miraculous preservation of it, as the
" child is supposed to be brought there by that bird of
" prey. Besides, I cannot find, with any show of pro-
" bability, that any of the family of Stanley ever
" assumed the ' Eagle and Child' for their crest before

" the union of the family of Lathom and Stanley, so
" that consequently there must be some special and
" peculiar view or occasion for the assumption of that
" crest by the Stanleys, rather than that taken by
" their common ancestor, Sir Thomas Lathom."

CHAPTER XII

THE following narrative of facts will explain itself, and serve to show why an additional chapter has been rendered necessary. Almost at the very moment when the foregoing pages were about to issue from the press, the Earl of Derby felt himself compelled, owing to continued indisposition, to resign the dignified and responsible office of Prime Minister. The announcement was received throughout the country, as well as by every political party in Parliament, with sentiments of the most profound regret. It was on the evening of Tuesday, February 25th, 1868, that the noble Earl's retirement was communicated to both Houses of Parliament. In the House of Lords it was made by the Earl of Malmesbury, in the following graceful and appropriate terms :—

"It is my duty," he said, "to inform your lord-" ships that the Earl of Derby has, from failing health,

" felt himself obliged to tender his resignation to her
" Majesty, and that her Majesty has been graciously
" pleased to send for the Right Hon. the Chancellor
" of the Exchequer, and to give him power to form a
" Government, if possible. It must be a subject of
" great pain to all, on whichever side of the House
" you sit, when you see an eminent statesman obliged
" to recede from public life, and the management of
" public affairs, not from any of those chances and
" changes of political life to which we are all accus-
" tomed, and cheerfully resign ourselves, but from
" failing health, which takes him as it were before
" his time from amongst us, and deprives us of his
" advice and ability. If this is painful to noble lords
" opposite, as I know it must be, how much more
" must it be to those friends who have served under
" him, as I have done, for so many years, and have
" sat by him through so many dreary years of Oppo-
" sition. There is one consolation, however, for us,
" under the circumstances. Although we may regret
" that we should be deprived of his presence from
" the cause which I have described, at the same time
" we have hope that the rest which he proposes to
" give himself, will restore him to us in greater
" strength, so that, at all events, we shall have again
" the advantage of his ability and eloquence."

The tribute paid to the retiring Premier, by Earl
Russell, who rose immediately on the Earl of

Malmesbury resuming his seat, testified to the respect and esteem in which the late head of the Government was held by those politically opposed to him, as well as by those of his own party.

"I may perhaps be permitted," said Earl Russell, "to express my sympathy with the noble Earl and "the rest of his colleagues, at the loss which they "have sustained in no longer having the Earl of "Derby at the head of her Majesty's Government. "Often as we have differed, and still differ, on many "public questions, I could not fail to regard him "with sentiments of respect and esteem, which his "great qualities were so well calculated to earn. "The confidence which has been bestowed upon him "by a great political party of this country is a proof "of the trust which he was so well calculated to "inspire. With regard to the eloquence with which "he stated his opinions, the records of Parliament "will bear immortal testimony. With respect to "all other matters which are public questions, history "must deal; but I trust, with the noble lord, that we "shall again see the Earl of Derby in the House, "and, although the state of his health, which is "much to be lamented, may prevent him from assum- "ing an official position, that we shall again hear "the clear and eloquent language (of which he is so "great a master) in which he is wont to express the "opinions which flowed from his great mind, so well

"calculated to inspire the respect and esteem of the
"House."

In the House of Commons the delicate duty fell
to the lot of the son of the late Premier himself.
Lord Stanley conveyed the intelligence to the House
in the following brief and characteristically modest
language :—

"Sir, I have to announce to the House, and I
"do it with feelings of deep regret, that Lord Derby,
"in consequence of the state of his health, which,
"although improving, is still such as to render abso-
"lute repose from business necessary for a consider-
"able time to come, has felt it his duty to tender to
"her Majesty his resignation of the office which he
"holds, and her Majesty has been pleased to accept
"the resignation so tendered."   Lord Stanley having
stated that Mr. Disraeli was engaged in the formation
of a ministry, then moved the adjournment of the
House, on which, Mr. Gladstone, the leader of the
Opposition, rose and paid the following appropriate
tribute to the noble Earl who had thus felt himself
compelled to retire from his position as the head of
the Government: "So far as regards the motion for
"adjournment," said Mr. Gladstone, "under present
"circumstances, I should not have thought that it
"called for a single word from myself, so obviously
"is it dictated by the propriety of the case.   But
"with reference to the special cause which the

"noble lord has, by a singular destiny, been called
"upon to be the person to announce to this House,
"I cannot help expressing, for myself, a regret which
"I am sure will be the universal sentiment, that a
"career so long, so active, and in so many respects
"so distinguished and remarkable as that of his
"father, should have been brought to a close by the
"failure of his bodily health and strength."

The Earl of Derby's retirement from public life,
and the universal sympathy felt for his lordship by
an admiring nation, invests with more than ordinary
interest anything bearing either directly or indirectly
on the event, and his lordship's remarks at a Conservative banquet at Manchester, on the 17th of October,
1867, at which the Earl and his colleagues were
entertained in celebration of the passing of the Reform
Bill, may here be most appropriately introduced.
Singularly enough, his lordship, in the course of one
of those eloquent speeches which he has often
delivered, pointedly alluded to a rumour then in
circulation, that he contemplated retiring from public
life. In reference to the rumour in question, his
lordship said:—"I have not the slightest idea of
"doing so. At a critical period like the present, I
"should feel that it would be an act of base
"dereliction of duty to my Sovereign, and those who
"honour me by giving me their support, if I were to
"shrink from the responsibility attaching to my

"present position. At my time of life, and with the
"increasing frequency of those attacks which from
"time to time oblige me to retire from public service,
"it is impossible for me to look forward to any
"lengthened service, but I have no present intention
"of relinquishing the office which I hold by the
"favour of my Sovereign, and the support of the
"great Conservative party. Whenever I do retire
"from that office, I trust that I shall have the satis-
"faction of doing so with the conviction that I have
"done my duty honestly and faithfully to the country
"at large; that I have not allowed political dif-
"ferences to interfere with personal friendship; and
"above all, that in no respect have I forfeited the
"good opinion and esteem of that great and influential
"party—never more great and influential than at the
"present moment—which has honoured me with its
"confidence for the last few years."

His references to public questions on the same
occasion, more particularly the Reform Act, and his
advent for the third time to power, are especially
deserving of record:—"Undertaking," he said "the
"duties and responsibilities of office, I felt I must
"look to the position in which I stood. That Reform,
"even if I had wished it, could have been postponed
"or defeated, was out of the question. To have
"brought forward a measure short of that brought
"forward by the late Government would equally

"have subjected me to ignominious discomfiture ; and
"believing that in this case boldness was safety, I felt
"that the only course to be pursued, if the concurrence
"of the great Conservative party could be obtained,
"was to make so large and liberal a concession of the
"elective franchise as that, resting upon a sound and
"definite principle, it should be a permanent obstacle
"to any attempt to disturb that principle.   It is a
"matter of the merest gratitude on my part to say
"that to the Conservative party I am deeply indebted
"for the manner in which they placed their entire
"confidence in myself and those associated with me,
"and for their concurrence in the large and extensive
"measure which we felt it our duty to propose.   Nay,
"more, when under the apprehension of losing three
"valued colleagues, we were induced to depart from
"our original intention, and to propose a bill less
"extensive in its character, it was not less by the
"objections of the Conservative than of the Liberal
"party that we were led to abandon the minor
"proposition, and recur to the larger and in-
"finitely more satisfactory measure which I am
"happy to say, has become the law of the land.
"And now, what is to be the result of this great
"measure ?   It is a serious question, and one well
"deserving of the grave attention of all those who
"are interested in the well-being of the country.   I
"am told that I used an imprudent expression—

" perhaps I did—in saying that this measure was to a
" certain extent a leap in the dark. It was; it is ;
" and it would be impossible to extend the electoral
" franchise to very large bodies of our fellow country-
" men with absolute certainty as to the manner in
" which they would use that franchise, not having the
" knowledge, which it is impossible to obtain, of the
" number entitled to exercise it. But, as I said before,
" I think that in this case boldness was safety, and I
" will add that the experience I acquired during the
" cotton famine of the very eminent and excellent
" qualities of the working men, especially in this dis-
" trict, led me to form such an opinion of their intelli-
" gence and reasonableness, and sound sense, and
" absence from personal and social prejudices, to
" believe that they could, without danger, be entrusted
" with a share in the administration of the country.
" I believe that what are called the working classes,
" which, I think, might be more properly described as
" the wage-paid classes of this country—those who
" depend upon weekly or monthly wages—are sound
" at heart and to the core. I have the greatest
" possible confidence in their loyalty to the throne and
" the institutions of the country. I believe that if—I
" will not say the person of the Sovereign—but the
" throne were threatened, they would rise as one man
" to protect it. I believe they are deeply attached to
" the institutions of the country. I believe that

" though many of them are not members of her com-
" munion, they respect and do not desire to subvert
" the Established Church of this country—a church,
" which I may be permitted to say, is of all establish-
" ments known upon the face of the earth most tolerant
" and most liberal, which gives the greatest latitude to
" its own members—a latitude, which, I am afraid, has
" of late times been rather abused—a church which is
" not only tolerant, but which cordially welcomes the
" assistance of its dissenting brethren in their common
" struggles against vice, and ignorance, and infidelity,
" I believe that the working classes have a deep res-
" pect for the old-established families of this country,
" and I do not believe that they desire to alter the
" constitution of the House of Lords, representing as
" it does hereditary rights and privileges, but recruited
" as it is year by year, from the ranks of the commu-
" nity. I believe further that the working classes enter-
" tain a deep respect for the legislative wisdom of the
" House of Commons, and that respect will be only
" deepened by their accession to privileges from which
" they have been hitherto debarred. I claim that du-
" ring the whole course of my political and private life
" I have been and continue to be, the friend and well-
" wisher of the working classes, and I think I know
" those classes well enough, and more especially in
" this immediate neighbourhood to know that there
" is nothing they wish so much as plain speak-

"ing and straightforward dealing. I will, therefore,
"in the presence of many of them—and I hope my
"words may reach many who are not present—venture
"to warn them against one danger which I foresee as a
"possible consequence of the great measure of Reform
"which has just been passed. Apprehensions are en-
"tertained that the working men will not be satisfied
"with exercising that political influence to which they
"will be entitled, but that they will be disposed to
"lend themselves as dupes to designing persons who
"may endeavour to cajole them with ideas of returning
"representatives to Parliament who will make loud
"professions of being the only friends of the working
"classes, and of going into Parliament to promote
"legislative measures intended to conduce to their
"welfare. Now, I believe there never was a Parlia-
'ment more disposed than the present to look to the
"interests of the working classes, and to consult their
"benefit. I can only hope that the next Parliament
"may be equally desirous to effect that object, and
"equally acquainted with the best mode of carrying
"it into effect. But, as an earnest and sincere friend,
"speaking with the deepest conviction, I warn the
"working classes not to be led away by the flattering
"delusions of men who will tell them they can induce
"Parliament to pass measures of exceptional legisla-
"tion for their special and immediate benefit. They
"could not, I hope, induce any Parliament to pass such

" measures, and if they were passed, the working men
" would find it the greatest injury that could be done
" to them."

It has already been stated that the noble Earl's
retirement called forth the deepest expressions of
regret from all classes and parties. The organs of
public opinion, both in the metropolis and in the
provinces were loud in his praises, and the following
tribute from the leading metropolitan diurnal, is only
one amongst many others breathing a kindred spirit
and feeling:—" So brilliant a political leader will not
" pass into the retirement which we trust he will
" long enjoy, without many attempts to estimate his
" services, and to define the influence which he
" exercised upon his most eminent contemporaries.
" The chief feature in his life is, that his power and
" popularity have been due more to his character and
" genius than to any positive achievements in states-
" manship. He has passed from the political stage
" without fulfilling any one of the grand ideas that
" fed the young fancies of the last generation. He
" has not been the heaven-sent statesman, to breast
" with his single persistency the raging element of
" revolution and conquest; he has not been the
" heaven-sent reformer, to point out with steady hand
" the true path of progress; he has not been mighty
" to originate and create; he has only assisted, not
" once, but many times, to bring his friends into the

"port they had most avoided and deprecated. Yet
"it would not be easy to name any one who has
"fulfilled with more distinction and success so many
"of the various parts expected in the composition of
"a modern British statesman, or gentleman of birth
"and position. Had he been only a scholar, or only
"an English landowner, or only an Irish proprietor,
"or only an administrator, or only a debater, or only
"a maker of laws, or only the leader of a party, or
"nothing more than the chief of his family, he would
"be a man of no common distinction in each of those
"characters. There is no man who could preside
"over a university with such authority and com-
"petency; nay, when learned doctors were humbly
"craving leave to say what they had to say in their
"mother tongue, Lord Derby could do this with
"perfect facility in good classical Latin. Fresh from
"the University, he proved a match for the great
"Irish agitator. He went great lengths in Reform,
"and the ensuing train of Liberal measures, insomuch
"as to leave his mark on that boisterous passage.
"But he had a conscience always in reserve; and
"although he suffered for a time, it stood him in
"good stead continually. One side could not dispute
"his good deeds, the other could not doubt his
"motives and intentions. Some important measures
"bear his name. In many a great crisis he has been
"a prominent personage, several times the expected

" deliverer.   He has been a valuable friend to both of
" the Irish churches, and to both of the great parties in
" the political world.   He now passes from political
" life with thanks, regrets, and expectations on all
" sides."

Since his speech at Manchester, in October last,
his lorship has not appeared in his public or political
character, excepting in connexion with the following
letter on his retirement, addressed to the Earl of
Dartmouth, Chairman of the National Union of
Conservative and Constitutional Associations :—

" St. James's-square, March 27, 1868.

" My Lord,—I have to acknowledge, with the
" liveliest gratitude, the address which your lordship
" has done me the honour of transmitting to me on
" behalf of the National Union, and the numerous
" Constitutional Associations whose names are annexed,
" kindly expressing their regret at my retirement
" from office, and their hope that I should still be
" enabled to take a part in the political business of
" the country.

" It was not without a pang, and only under a con-
" viction of the absolute necessity of the step, that
" I found myself compelled to ask permission to with-
" draw from the service of a Sovereign to whose
" gracious favours I am so deeply indebted ; and to
" sever my official connexion with a party which for so

" many years has honoured me with its confidence,
" and for many members of which I entertain a per-
" sonal as well as a political regard.   It was, however,
" very satisfactory to me to be empowered to transfer
" the office which I had the honour of holding, to one
" whose co-operation and friendship I had enjoyed for
" more than twenty years, and who, I am persuaded,
" will prove himself not unmindful of those great
" constitutional principles which it has been the study
" of my life to uphold, and to which, so far as my
" health will permit, I shall not cease to give my
" earnest though unofficial support.—I have the hon-
" our to be, my Lord, your obliged and faithful
" servant,"   " DERBY."

* We cannot more appropriately close our narrative
than by recording the testimony of an able and
influential publication, politically opposed to the distinguished subject of our notice.   Speaking of the
Earl of Derby's retirement, the writer says :—" In all
" the private relations of life, and as a public man
" apart from politics, Lord Derby has justly earned
" the confidence of men of all political opinions.
" His conduct during the cotton famine was such as
" to entitle him to the gratitude of his fellow-country-
" men and to the respect of the world.   Nor was this
" a solitary or even a rare instance of his benevolence.

" He has always been true to his order, by connecting
" it with the well-being of all other classes of society.
" Of his intellectual qualities it is unnecessary to
" speak, as he has long stood in the first rank of
" English orators. As a scholar he is surpassed by
" few Englishmen, perhaps by none who have not
" made scholarship the whole object of their lives.
" We are quite sure that the whole of his countrymen
" will join in sincerely hoping that his life may be
" spared for many years, and that in the company of
" his family, and his books, and his performance of
" whatever public duties his strength may enable
" him to discharge, he will spend the last years of his
" life in tranquillity and in happiness."